"Our world can convince us we need to do "big" things for God. But we serve a Savior who came to a tiny manger in a small town to live a simple life of uncommon obedience. Dolly's words help us stop striving and instead lean into the grace, love and intimacy we truly need and only God can give."

—**Holley Gerth**, Wall Street Journal Bestselling Author of *You're Already Amazing*

"*7 Days of Soul Care* is a compact and powerful resource for life change. It is the voice of the wise friend offering counsel, providing real-life encouragement, and whispering the truth of your identity in Christ. This guide provides the practical tools you need to step forward and move deeper in accepting and living out the freedom Christ says is yours."

—**Jennifer J. Camp**, author of *Breathing Eden*

"Through creative stories, thoughtful questions, and rich prayers, Dolly Lee's *7 Days of Soul Care* kick-starts a lifetime habit of reflection and study for someone longing for something deeper with God. Lee clearly longs for readers to see themselves through the eyes of our extraordinary God."

—**Ann Kroeker**, writing coach and author of *The Contemplative Mom*

"Dolly is a gentle, knowledgeable guide. This grace-filled book captures the essential steps to escape shame and persistent unworthiness in the Christian life."

—**Mick Silva**, Author Coach and Editor

"Artist, learner, and listener Dolly Lee brings together her transformed brokenness, heightened awareness, and shared empathy in *7 Days of Soul Care*, a devotional about God and self, suffering and grace, Scripture and prayer. Freeing and renewing, this carefully crafted passing on of life lessons, questions, and inspirations will grow you in knowing and connecting with God.

—**Monica Sharman**, Editor and Author of *Behold the Beauty: An Invitation to Bible Reading*

"Like the layers of color on an artist's canvas, Dolly Lee's words in *7 Days of Soul Care* display a depth of beauty and wisdom. She graciously invites us on a journey of reflection and renewal as we discover our exceptionalism, born from an intimate connection with an exceptional God. The end result is a masterpiece that celebrates everything God created us to be. You will love this book!"

—**Lisa Murray,** author of *Peace For A Lifetime*

Social media's incessant demands and the whirlwind of busyness we've embraced have done nothing but distract us from the care and feeding of our weary, parched souls. You'll find Dolly Lee's *7 Days of Soul* Care to be a lovely spiritual mini-retreat, a nurturing, Christ-centered guidebook you'll return to again and again. Come thirsty!

—**Linda R. Stoll**, M.S., CLC, BCPC, Board Certified Pastoral Counselor, Certified Life Coach, LindaStoll.net

7 Days of Soul Care

A Guide to Letting God Do the

Extraordinary with Your Ordinary

Dolly M. Lee

ISBN 978-0-9980547-0-4

For Brian
with love

"It is ingrained in us that we have to do exceptional things for God—but we do not. We have to be exceptional in the ordinary things of life, and holy on the ordinary streets, among ordinary people—and this is not learned in five minutes."

—Oswald Chambers, *My Utmost For His Highest*

CONTENTS

INTRODUCTION

"Great things are not done by impulse,
but by a series of small things brought
together."

—Vincent van Gogh[1]

God, the Master Artist, designed each
of us as unique masterpieces (see
Ephesians 2:10).

I gazed at Vincent van Gogh's iconic painting *Irises* at The Getty Center in Los Angeles. Van Gogh applied paint in small brush strokes, layering diverse colors to create texture. He used blue paint in various hues and thicknesses to capture each iris in a different stage of bloom across the canvas. Undulating waves of green made the irises' leaves dance. He also added a little white and yellow in the center of several flowers. A single white iris

2

contrasts with an impasto of different shades of orange paint forming bright marigolds in the upper left corner.

When I examined Van Gogh's small paint strokes up close, they looked pointless. I couldn't see the big picture. But when I stepped away, I saw how his small strokes came together to become this masterpiece *Irises*. Small strokes of brown, red, white, and taupe paint made the ground come alive.

The following quote by Oswald Chambers reminds me the small strokes of my everyday life painted with God the Master Artist creates a masterpiece from my life's canvas. "It is ingrained in us that we have to do exceptional things for God—but we do not. We have to be exceptional in the ordinary things of life, and holy on the ordinary streets, among ordinary people—and this is not learned in five minutes." —Oswald Chambers, *My Utmost For His Highest*[2]

What does it mean to be, as Oswald Chambers wrote, "exceptional in the ordinary things of life, and holy on the ordinary streets, among ordinary people"? *I define "exceptional" as connecting with our extraordinary God to be our best.* The key is connecting with God so we can rely on his unlimited resources. I don't define "best" to mean better than others.

Rather by "best," I mean "more fully myself as God created." God created each of us with different gifts and personalities so each of us has a different "best." My "best" isn't better than your best, and your "best" isn't better than mine. In God's eyes, each person's best has a distinct and unique worth. Each is celebrated.

This journey to become exceptional begins when we connect with God so his love flows into and through us. Because God's Spirit dwells within his children, we can trust that whatever our daily routine involves—whether in the kitchen, the boardroom, or the classroom—is sacred. And each person we encounter is sacred. He or she bears the image of God no matter how hidden or distorted the image may be. When we engage with our extraordinary God in our ordinary, we become exceptional in the ordinary because *his Spirit is with us and within us.*

Likewise, as we do ordinary things, like faithfully working at a job, practicing acts of kindness, or raising children—the brush strokes of daily life viewed close–up—it can appear as if nothing great is being created. No work of art seems to unfold in the ordinary, small details of our lives. But what if we did our ordinary things with our extraordinary

4

God, till we learn to be "exceptional in the ordinary things of life"? What if we kept practicing being exceptional each day? We paint with God as we create layer after layer of love and faithfulness onto the canvas of our lives, our communities, and our world. And as we connect with God in our ordinary, we will create a masterpiece with God.

And it does *not* happen in five minutes.

I write this book because I believe we create great art with our lives as we daily partner with God over a lifetime. This is how we let God do the extraordinary with our ordinary. Together.

May this book kick-start your process of being exceptional in the ordinary things of life, forming a masterpiece.

Structure for each of the seven days

Each day for seven days, I share a biblical truth through a **story**, followed by **questions and thoughts** for you to reflect on and discover how you best connect with God. Please don't feel compelled to answer each question. It is better to answer one question thoughtfully than to race through and answer all of them. Feel free to return to the questions when you have more time.

Each day ends with a **prayer**. Prayer is the fuel

that drives the engine of lasting transformation because it connects us with God's presence and power. But prayer can also occur without words as we walk, work, and love. Or we may be silent in God's loving presence as a way of being and listening for his voice of love.

You may want to read alone or in a group. From my years of participating (and sometimes leading) in small groups, I discovered I usually gain additional insights from group discussion because we each have different strengths and struggles in our relationship with God. Each person in the group enabled me to see God in a new way. The group discussion often came after I first processed alone with God.

If you fall behind, no worries. Simply begin where you left off.

Thank you for joining me in doing a series of small things for seven days so we can let God do the extraordinary with our ordinary. As we daily seek God, we will become exceptional (defined as connecting with our extraordinary God to be our best) in the ordinary things of life. In the day–to–day, as we paint on the canvas of our lives with each thought, word or action, we can't always see where our little strokes will lead or what kind of painting we create with God, the Master Artist. It is only after reflection and the distance of time, we can see the art that God and we paint with our lives.

We partner with God to create beautiful art with each daily brush stroke. As we paint, more beauty will be revealed. Let's begin, together.

DAY 1

Know God, Know Yourself

"We can never know who or what we
are till we know at least something of
what God is."

—A.W. Tozer

In June 2015, a woman found a forgotten, old computer belonging to her deceased husband in their garage. The computer was bulky and heavy compared to today's sleek models. She donated the clunky, outdated computer to an electronics-recycling center in Northern California. She didn't know its true worth. But someone at the recycling center did. The rare Apple 1 sold for $261,470 at auction. She didn't leave contact information, so the center couldn't give her half of its sale price, or $130, 735.[3]

Unlike current Apple products, the Apple I

wasn't mass–produced, so the Apple I's high value came because Steve Job's hands probably helped create it. But the woman considered neither its worth as a machine, which appeared worthless, nor its worth based on its maker. Just as the woman didn't know the Apple I's true value, we too can undervalue our worth and the worth of others because we aren't considering the Creator who made us—and his heart of love. Similarly, we can forget our true identity and value as God's beloved children. For example, we can base our worth on externals instead of on the *real* us hidden behind skin, hair, clothes, and maybe a less than sleek exterior. And we know how quickly the value of an item can change with trends. If we saw the real person God sees, we might remember God created each of us as unique masterpieces with distinct and different gifts (see Ephesians 2:10)—each person valued and valuable.

God as Creator

God can create something out of nothing, order out of chaos. In Genesis 1, we read how God created the heavens, the earth, the sea, and all living creatures. He created us in his image; we were God's final creation. After creating humans, God declared his creation *very good*.

Before our parents and the world determined our worth, God saw each of us and said, "very good," despite our imperfections.

In some families, parents may have said "very good," when you aced an exam or scored the most points in a game. You were at least seen and acknowledged. In healthier families, you were declared "very good" if you tried your best regardless of outcome. But in God's family, he declared you "very good" simply because he created you. It doesn't mean everything you and I do is "very good," because God sent Jesus to rescue us from sin's dominion. But it does mean God sees you and me as *inherently worthy* apart from our performance.

God doesn't love you more when you win awards or the game, and God doesn't love you less if you fail.

Even after Adam and Eve rebelled against God, God didn't give up on them. In Genesis 3:15, God promised a Messiah who would overcome the serpent who lied to Eve. The serpent caused Eve to doubt God's goodness. Mistrust replaced trust. God's love is extraordinary because he didn't abandon Adam and Eve when they betrayed his trust. Instead, God sought to restore and redeem humankind through Jesus.

God gave Adam and Eve (and us) the gift of free choice. And when they used it to betray him, God pursued them to restore their relationship to him. And he does the same for us. Extraordinary. Unexpected. Likewise, God doesn't abandon us when we turn from him. He waits for us, like the loving father in The Parable of The Prodigal Son, to return home. We explore this parable more in Day 6.

God loved us at our sin–worst (see Romans 5:8), so he isn't shocked by what we do as revealed by our natural tendency to think first of ourselves in most, if not all, matters. A child usually doesn't need to be taught to consider only his or her desires. For example, we ask (sometimes unaware), as part of our decision-making, "What's in it for me?" before we consider what would be best for another person. Of course, we consider our needs; I only highlight our first thought tends to be about ourselves. In contrast, God loved us in our selfishness and rebellion.

It took many years for the truth of God's unconditional love to break past the walls in my heart I'd built for protection. Once I opened myself to receive more of God's love, it became more and more of a life–transforming reality. Slowly over the years, I sensed God's love as a felt-experience and not merely an abstract theological concept. Our deepest truths are not merely propositional but also deeply felt and personal.

God revealed his unconditional love for us by loving us at our sin–worst and giving us a way to be reconciled to God through the life, death and resurrection of his Son, Jesus Christ (see Romans 5:6–12). God desired relationship with us. When we know God loves us unconditionally, it gives us the grace and space to become all God created us to be—exceptional (which means to connect with God to be our best). And when we discover who God is and our truest identity as beloved by God, then we become exceptional in the ordinary things of life. Step by step.

Suffering can affect our view of God

But our belief about suffering (and the suffering itself) can distort our view of God as loving and also how we perceive ourselves. If God allowed us to suffer, then maybe we're not worth much because if God loved us then he wouldn't have allowed us to suffer.

In his book The *Good and Beautiful God*, James

Bryan Smith shares how his first daughter, Madeline, was born with a rare chromosomal disorder. Defying the doctors' prognoses, she survived birth but weighed only a few pounds, had a heart defect, and couldn't keep food down. After two years, she died.

Before and after her death, people said many insensitive and hurtful things to James and his wife. One pastor friend asked James if he and his wife had sinned and intimated God was punishing them. Several people made incorrect theological statements, such as, "I guess God just wanted her in heaven more than He wanted her here."[4]

The truth is, we can't really know God's purposes, as illustrated by Job's perspective on his suffering. In the book of Job, God answered Job's questions with more questions (see Job 38–41). Did God ask Job questions because God's ways are mysterious and beyond our comprehension? I don't know. God didn't answer Job's questions, but he didn't condemn Job for asking them. We can be comforted, knowing God welcomes our honest questions and doubts. God did, however, rebuke Job's discouraging friends and their bad theology (see Job 42:7–9).

James Bryan Smith rejected his friend's narrative

of a God who looks to punish (which differs from correction out of love), or of a God who is capricious and small. Instead, Smith pointed to how Jesus answered the question in the story of a man who was born blind in John 9. In response to the disciples' question of whose sin caused the man's blindness, Jesus declared, "It was not that this man sinned, or his parents, but that the works of God might be displayed in him" (John 9:3).

Smith didn't let his daughter or his own suffering derail his view of a loving God, because he knew Jesus *also* experienced deep suffering. And as he processed his grief, Smith came to a deeper knowledge of himself and God. In his book *The Good and Beautiful God*, he discussed God's character and why he still found God to be trustworthy and good despite the suffering he, his wife, and his daughter experienced.

The rest of my book is about knowing ourselves better in light of our relationship with God, so I wanted to first address what many struggle with in their relationship with God—whether they are aware of it or not. I didn't know how much past pain unconsciously affected my view of God till I was much older. I talk more about this later.

The more I know our extraordinary God, then

the more I can be exceptional (*defined as connecting with our extraordinary God to be my best*) in all the ordinary things of my life. I won't seek to connect with God if I don't trust him. And trust comes from shared experiences—the daily and the profound. Because of unacknowledged past pain, I found it difficult to fully trust God until I shared my pain with God and he responded with compassion instead of condemnation. When I learned I could trust God with my gritty unedited emotions, it became easier for me to also trust him with other areas of my heart and life.

Safe people (who modeled God's love) were also part of my process of growing in trust.

For the past few years, I have asked God for the grace to trust him more. And slowly, my trust has grown.

I learned to connect more often with God *in* my ordinary moments as I washed dishes, taught, wrote, parented, and related to my husband, our daughter, and friends. I connected with God through talking with him, songs, and memorized Scripture. Learning to listen for God's gentle whisper in silence and solitude is also another practice I've been cultivating. As I learned to connect with God more consistently each day, I found I could be my best more and more. I began to discover the joy of being exceptional in the ordinary things of life.

Even when I fail or sin, I'm learning to connect with God by quickly asking for forgiveness and grace instead of wallowing in shame and condemnation.

Being exceptional begins when we connect with God. It has taken me decades to learn: relationship with God begins first with our "being" and *not* with our "doing." God values our presence more than our gifts. And I relearn this truth every day in deeper and new ways.

My prayer for you: may you discover more and more the joy of doing your ordinary with our extraordinary God so he can do the extraordinary with your ordinary.

Journal Questions

"For the word of God is living and
active, sharper than any two–edged
sword, piercing to the division of soul
and of spirit, of joints and of marrow,
and discerning the thoughts and
intentions of the heart."

—Hebrews 4:12 (ESV)

1. Who or what influenced your perspective of God's character? Could you ask God to reveal what experiences affected your view of him? Was it a person? Experience? Media? Book? How does that message about God compare to the God revealed by Jesus and the Bible (God's revelation to us via different people across hundreds of years)?

2. If you wrote quickly, how would you answer these questions:

Who is God?

How does God view you—the real (unedited)

you?

3.   Do you struggle to believe God wants to know you and wants what is best for you?

Read Psalm 16 aloud several times. How is God portrayed in Psalm 16? Is there one verse or phrase you can draw or write on an index card or on your phone's notes as a reminder? Ask God's Spirit to reveal truth about how God sees you and to replace any lies with truth.

4.   What images impact you when you read John 19 or Isaiah 53 aloud? When you contemplate how Jesus suffered, how do you feel? Does it change how you see God and his love for you? Do you notice any resistance to God's love? Ask God to show you how to overcome your resistance to believing he loves you so much.

5.   Are you willing to be open to letting God reveal his love for you?

The Bible describes God's love using the Greek word agapé, which means God's love doesn't depend on our worthiness or on us doing anything for him. Are you willing to let go of preconceived ideas of what God is like? Ask God to reveal himself to you, and ask for the eyes to truly see and experience his love for you. Will you ask God for the grace to believe and receive his love for you?

6.   What would happen if you were willing to release the images and ideas that are inconsistent with how God is revealed through Jesus and the Bible?

Ask God for the grace to see him as he really is. Whenever I have prayed this, God has shown me how many of my false images of him are based on faulty human models of love. It has taken decades to recognize and dismantle many of my false and subconscious views of God.

7.   Can you trust God with your hurt, anger and pain? What is one honest thing you can tell God today?

Sometimes it is hard to see God because all we can see is our hurt, pain and disappointment. I know it can be scary but whenever I've done this,

God has come with his love. *God can heal what we acknowledge as real before him.* God invites us to pour out our hearts to him because he wants to be our refuge (see Psalm 62:8). God is like a loving friend or parent who invites us to sit and share our story with him. God longs to hear from us.

Prayer

When seeking to heed God's call, we
can't separate the inner from the outer
life.

—Mark Labberton, *Called*

Dear God,

I confess I don't know you as well as I claim sometimes.

Thank you for how Jesus was a man acquainted with sorrow but also a man of joy. You long to walk with me though the valleys, on the peaks, and in my ordinary moments.

Forgive me when I form you in my own image and create an idol from my idea of you instead of the real you revealed through Jesus and the Bible.

Forgive me when I make you small and someone I can manipulate by my actions.

Please give me the grace to believe you are bigger, more powerful, more gracious, and more loving than I can imagine (see Ephesians 3:14–21).

Please give me a holy imagination.

I ask for the grace to experience more of you, your ways, and your heart, as I read the Bible and look at your creation. Thank you for how seeds grow, how the sun rises and sets, and how billions of stars (I can't see) exist and hint at your beauty and grandeur.

Please provide friends to accompany me on this journey of knowing you more intimately.

Thank you that as I know you more, I will also know myself better because you created me. Please give me the grace to be exceptional in the ordinary things of my life to your glory and for our joy.

In your Son's name, amen.

DAY 2

Embrace Your True Worth

"All that God wanted man to do was to
believe in him. What a man [or woman]
believes moves and rules his [or her]
whole being, enters into him [or her],
and becomes part of his [or her] very
life."

—Andrew Murray

For many years, I didn't believe God truly delighted in how he created me with my unique strengths. During my formative years, the message I received was my desires and dreams were not to be expressed, seen, or heard. Like the air I breathed, this message was imprinted on my soul without my awareness. As a result, I didn't allow myself to develop as a writer or a reader. For many years, I rarely allowed myself to read fiction for pleasure.

Instead I mostly read nonfiction because it informed and served a purpose, such as becoming a better parent. All of these beliefs operated in stealth mode until a triggering event (more in Day 5) began a long, slow process of becoming conscious of how much I needed healing and restoration.

I've learned what we believe about our worth is one of the biggest determinants of how we live our lives. If we don't believe what God says about our worth as shown by what God paid for us through Christ's life, death, and resurrection, then we won't eat well or exercise, or nurture our gifts, and we'll put up with abusive behavior instead of enforcing healthy boundaries.

Over the past five years, I stretched myself by writing a blog. I never thought I would blog because it was *too* public. I didn't put my name or my photo on the website (http://soulstops.com) for almost a year. When I hit "publish" on a post, I felt like I wore a big target on my back. Because of past experiences, I feared rejection and judgment. But each time I wrote, I practiced dying to perfectionism and my fears. I practiced trusting God's love covered my imperfections and my fears. Blogging gradually became less scary as I made new friends.

Discover our strengths and struggles

We can't be exceptional—*defined as connecting with our extraordinary God to be our best*—unless we believe it is worth discovering who we really are, which includes our God-given strengths. God desires to connect with all aspects of our personhood (the good and the ugly). And once sin entered humanity, we all have an ugly side. We need to know who are (in all of our glorious complexity) if we want to be our individual best—defined as "more fully myself as God created." We can't be our best if we don't know what our best is. Being our best is not about comparison.

God gifted us each differently so each person's best is unique and valuable.

Those of us who have spent years trying to fit our circle into the square expectation key people wanted us to be, have lost touch with our hearts—we need to feel again, and believe. We will take the time and effort to learn how God wired us if we believe our extraordinary worth. For me, growth and change came in small, incremental steps.

God declares we are wonderfully made and he created each of us with unique gifts and talents (Psalm 139:13–16). We don't need to be like someone else. We only need to be ourselves. (And I know this can be hard but we can ask God for the grace to believe he delights in us.) We must believe who God created us is good. We're enough because God is enough.

Some are born leaders, some are happiest serving in the background, some love to write, others to innovate, and still others feel great joy when they feed others with food or encouragement. We each have a unique role to play. No role—however big or small—is unimportant. *When we truly believe our extraordinary God for our identity, we will believe we're worth taking care of.* For me, it means exercising so I have energy to love my family well, write, teach, and do whatever God calls me to do in my community.

Whenever I shop at a grocery store, glossy magazine covers tell me I am worth more if my relationships are secure and if I look sexy and youthful. And when I was in school, grades were what some used to determine worth for a scholarship or a job. Yet God doesn't base our worth on our performance, position, or possessions.

There is nothing wrong with performing well or owning nice things. What hurts is when we base our worth or another's worth on such temporal values. Moreover, other people, praise, or possessions will never fill our soul's deep need for unconditional eternal love, which only God can provide.

God wants us to be exceptional, but he doesn't want us to base our identity on our performance as determined by us or external markers. God doesn't want us to feel worthy if we're doing well or to feel unworthy when we're not. In God's eyes, our worth doesn't go up and down like the stock market. I'm still learning to live more and more into this truth.

So often we can be deceived into not recognizing our true worth because we listen to our culture's focus on outward indicators, such as appearance, accomplishments, and attachments. We forget to look at ourselves from God's eternal and loving perspective. God doesn't look at externals but at our heart (see 1 Samuel 16:7). Our heart reveals who or what we love and who loves us. Will we receive and believe God's love for us? If we do, then we will believe we have inherent worth. When we believe our true identity as beloved, then we can be exceptional (connecting with our extraordinary God to be our best) in the ordinary things of our life.

Sometimes people or events break our hearts, making it hard for us to trust and believe God's love for us because of painful memories or trauma. God desires to heal us. Christ bears our suffering with us if we allow him to be part of our healing. Jesus suffered shame and abandonment on the cross so we would never be shamed and forsaken. We'll talk more about the condition of the heart in Day 4 of this book.

Believe God for our worth

How can we know our true worth? How can we experience the freedom that comes when we look beyond what we can see and measure?

When we read God's Word, the Bible, we learn our true worth from God's loving perspective. When we believe God for our worth, then we can walk in freedom from trying to create our own worth, or having someone else give it to us. We all know how easily feelings and perceptions shift, but how God sees us doesn't change with popular opinion or our circumstances (see Romans 8:31–39).

May God give us the grace to fully embrace our true worth as his beloved.

We can also ask God's Spirit to reveal to us the truth about ourselves. God's Spirit is like a mirror reflecting back to us the truth when we look to God. Yes, we see dimly now but one day we will see clearly through God's eyes of love (see 1 Corinthians 13:12).

People who see us through God's loving lens also open our eyes to our inherent worth. Friends help me to believe in myself when I cannot, or when I struggle. Similarly, I often see a friend's value when she cannot. We need each other.

We can ask God for the grace to believe his view of us as Beloved. The more we see ourselves as Beloved, then the more we can see others as also Beloved by God.

We have intrinsic worth

God (Trinity of God the Father, Jesus the Son, and the Spirit) created us in his image (see Genesis 1:26–27). God declared we have worth apart from anything we do or what has been done to us, because God imprinted his image on us.

God created us in his image and declared our creation as *very good*. Even in our brokenness, we still bear God's image—our value comes from our extraordinary Maker forming us (see Psalm 139:13–14). Remember how in Day 1, the woman didn't recognize the old, clunky Apple I had value due to its creation by Steve Jobs? Similarly, we have inherent worth apart from our appearance, or our behavior, or how another has treated us, because *God created us in love for love*. It is why God didn't give up on us and instead pursued us with a lover's heart (see Hosea 2). No matter how bad our actions, God forgives us if we seek forgiveness and change, which is the hard–to–wrap–the–mind–around truth. We may bear the scars from our choices but they don't define our worth in Christ. That's the scandalous grace and mercy of God's forgiveness in Christ (see Ephesians 2:4–10).

"Then God said, 'Let us make man [in Hebrew, this word translated "man" means "humans or mankind"] in our image, after our likeness....' [I]n the image of God he created him; male and female he created them" (Genesis 1:26a, 27). Male and female both bear God's image. One gender is *not* more valuable than another although some cultures believe otherwise.

How do you feel when you walk into a room and spot a friend whose face lights up when your eyes meet? Doesn't it make you smile and warm your heart? Well, God delights in you so much he sings over you (see Zephaniah 3:17). Imagine God composing a song especially for you. When our daughter was a baby, I sang to her as my arms cradled her close to my chest. She didn't need to impress me to earn my love. Simply her being was a gift. So it is with God's love for us. We exist and we're enough in God's eyes. God loves us because we're his.

Extraordinary—God looks at us with delight just because we're his.

God may not always delight in how I act but he always looks at the real me with delight.

It took decades for this truth—*God finds delight in my being apart from doing*—to become more of a felt truth and not merely an abstract intellectual belief. It was like admiring a photo of a chocolate cupcake versus eating it and letting my taste buds enjoy its sweetness. (God's love, of course, is infinitely superior to any cupcake.) God's love for me exists apart from what I do, but his love can't transform me until I allow it to enter my heart. A life of faith involves daily tasting God's goodness and love again and again (see Psalm 34:8).

As our bodies need daily sustenance, our souls need to daily take in God's Word, presence, and love.

God's extraordinary delight in us doesn't depend on our exceptional performance. We don't need to hit the winning home run, score the highest on a test, or have the most Facebook "friends." We don't need to jostle to the front of the line to prove we're lovable and worthy. When we rest in our true identity and worth in God, we can be exceptional in the ordinary things of life because we believe our worth is secure. And if we believe our worth is secure, we're free to love others without needing their affirmation to shore up our self–worth. We can stop hustling for love.

God isn't like a human parent who abandons a child physically or emotionally. Nor is God like a human lover who may turn on you when you're not as young, exciting, or as useful as when you first met. God keeps his promises. He is faithful like the perfect parent or spouse. God is the Good Shepherd who always cares and provides for his sheep (see Psalm 23). No single analogy can capture all the riches of God's character, but we can glimpse his magnificence and glory in the images provided in the Bible itself. We can spend a lifetime growing in intimacy with God and never exhaust the depth of his character.

Journal Questions

Everything created by God reflects his
glory in some way.

—Rick Warren, *The Purpose-Driven Life*

1.   What phrases or concepts resonate with you about God and how he values you when you read Psalm 139:1–18 aloud slowly, at least three times, or listen to it being read via Biblegateway.com's audio recording of certain translations (like ESV or The Message)?

Write them down or use them as a starting point to create art (draw, audio, or tactile etc.). Do what helps you to rest more in the truth of your intrinsic worth to God. Is there a song you can listen to that expresses this truth?

2.   What does God tell us through the Bible about our extraordinary worth? Read Matthew 6:25–34. Which image speaks to you of God's tender care

for you? The lilies? The sparrow? Meditate on it whenever you have a pause, such as when you're stuck in traffic or waiting in line.

3. Pick a Bible verse (or verses) to memorize and pray over in the morning, and continue to meditate on it throughout the day. How can you incorporate that verse (or verses) into your day? For example, today I prayed over Psalm 37:7. Every time stress and anxiety appeared, I prayed: "God, please give me the grace to rest in you and to wait patiently." Another option is a breath prayer, such as inhale "Grace," then you exhale, "to rest." What breath prayer can you create?

4. How do you feel knowing God invites all to become his children?

"But to all who did receive him [Jesus], who believed in his name, he gave the right to become the children of God, who were born, not of blood nor of the will of the flesh, nor of the will of man, but of God." (John 1:12–13 ESV)

5. Do you believe God is the Father who cheers your every effort to please him even if you fail? He doesn't expect perfection. He thinks about you constantly (see Psalm 139:17–18), and he will never ever abandon you (see Deuteronomy 31:8). How can you personalize the truth of these promises today? Some of us need to ask God to first heal our concept of him as father because we may have unconsciously patterned our view of God after a neglectful or abusive father. Even if we had loving fathers, they're still fallible. Ask the Holy Spirit to help you experience and believe God has a tender father's heart for you.

6. How do you respond to the following quote?

"To be nobody but yourself in a world
which is doing its best, night and day,
to make you everybody but yourself—
means to fight the hardest battle which
any human being can fight—and never
stop fighting.

—e.e. cummings

7. Do you ever struggle to become the person God created you to be? What beliefs or lies make it hard for you to believe you can become exceptional (connecting with our extraordinary God to be the best you)? What truth(s) can you replace the lie(s) with?

8. What comes naturally for you? What is one thing you can do to honor or celebrate how God designed you? Go for a run? Walk? Paint? Write? Sing? Organize? Lead? Encourage? Serve? Write software? Build? Bake? Clean?

9. Are you an introvert, an extrovert, or a mix of the two? How can you practice the freedom to live as our extraordinary God created you, so you can be exceptional in the ordinary things of life? Create time for solitude? Set aside time for community?

I speed walked through most of my life, only recently realizing God created me to be someone who needs time to slow down and process her thoughts and feelings. God made us each with different temperaments—all are needed. We need the quiet and the loud, the dreamers and the doers.

Ask God for the grace to see the goodness in how he created you. It might help to ask a good friend or a loved one what they see as unique about you. Many of us can see another person's gifts more easily than we can see our own. Or you can ask God to reveal your strengths and gifts. In 1999, I asked God to reveal how he designed me. This book is part of his unfolding answer to my prayer.

Prayer

"Prayer is the only entryway into
genuine self–knowledge. It is also the
main way we experience deep change—
the reordering of our loves."

—Timothy Keller, *Prayer*

Our Father God,

Thank you for giving me extraordinary worth because you created me in your image. Thank you for placing gifts inside of me. Help me to see and nurture those gifts. I ask for the grace to see myself as you do and to believe I am worth taking care of physically, spiritually, mentally, emotionally, and psychologically.

I confess I sometimes don't believe in my inherent worth. You love me apart from anything I can do or don't do. Forgive me when I doubt your love for me despite all you've done. Heal those wounds within that prevent me from fully receiving your love for me.

Learning to love myself is not selfish as you call

me to love my neighbor as myself.

Help me to experience as truth in the marrow of my soul: You love me unconditionally. *Nothing I do will cause you to love me more or less than you already do as shown in Christ's life, death, and resurrection.*

Thank you for loving me too much to let me continue in sinful and hurtful ways so you correct me. Please reorder my loves so I love you above all, including myself.

Please give me the grace to believe and receive your words of love instead of the lies declaring I need to be more and do more to earn your love and approval.

In Christ, I am made new (see Colossians 3:10). Help me to live more and more into my new identity in Christ.

In your Son's name, amen.

DAY 3

Know Jesus, Know God

"He [Jesus] is the radiance of the glory
of God and the exact imprint of his
nature…"

—Hebrews 1:3 (ESV)

In Day 1, we learned about how knowing God,
helps us to know ourselves better. Now we explore
how when we know Jesus, we will know God better.
When we see how Jesus interacted with people
when he lived on earth, we glimpse God's character.
The gospel according to John in the New Testament
presents stories and Jesus's words as a way to reveal
Jesus as the Son of God and Messiah. I share one of
my favorite stories as it focuses on one of John's
themes: Jesus is the Son of God, who embodies
grace and truth.

The woman caught in adultery[5]

She waited until her husband left, then quickly changed her clothes and slipped away to meet her lover. She and her lover's lips were locked and bodies entwined when men barged into the room. Her lover silently watched as the men dragged her out, barely clothed, onto the temple grounds. The scent of bodies, sweat, and animal sacrifices reached her nose. People stopped their chatter to stare.

She recognized the men as the town's religious leaders. How did they know about their secret meeting? They told no one, or at least she hadn't told anyone. She covered her body as best as she could while feeling the heat of many eyes on her bare skin.

The hustle and bustle of temple life stilled while the men asked a stranger, called Jesus, "Teacher, this woman has been caught in the act of adultery. Now in the Law Moses commanded us to stone such women. So what do you say?"

Quiet.

All eyes turned to where Jesus sat, teaching in the temple. The religious leaders confronted Jesus because they were testing him to discover a charge to bring against him.

How would Jesus respond to their challenge?

Jesus bent down and wrote in the dirt with his finger.

He continued to write and said nothing.

But the men could see.

The leaders kept asking with louder and more insistent voices that Jesus answer them.

What would Jesus do?

Finally, Jesus stood up and said, "Let him who is without sin among you be the first to throw a stone at her." Then he kneeled again and wrote on the dirt.

The silence felt like a heavy cloak, stifling in the heat.

Slowly, the leaders walked away, one by one, first the older men, then the younger, until she was alone with Jesus.

"Woman, where are they? Has no one condemned you?" he asked.

She replied, "No one, Lord."

And Jesus said, "Neither do I condemn you; go and from now on sin no more.

Jesus didn't do what anyone expected.

Instead of agreeing with the religious leaders who sought to punish her according to Mosaic Law by stoning her to death, Jesus extended grace to the woman. He gave her another chance. He didn't condemn her. But he also spoke truth when he called her actions "sin" and told her to stop. He also showed grace to the religious leaders because he gave them a way to bow out. Jesus, the *only* sinless one, didn't cast a stone. Later Jesus would be whipped and crucified for their sins and all of humanity's brokenness. Jesus bore our condemnation and fulfilled Mosaic law.

Jesus suffered hell (body, soul, and spirit) for us.

And when Jesus rose from the dead, he instituted a new covenant with both Jews and Gentiles (see Ephesians 3:6). He made us family.

Jesus embodied grace and truth (see John 1:17). He came to give people grace through forgiveness of their sins by his life, death, and resurrection. In grace, Jesus restored our relationship with a holy God (see Ephesians 2:4-9). Jesus lived the perfect life we could never live.

Jesus gave us the Spirit to empower us to live a new way—through connection to God instead of alienation. Think of the difference it makes when your phone is connected to a viable power source. Or have you ever wondered why your coffee maker wasn't working then realized it was unplugged?

Grace means Jesus restored our connection with God based on *his* good and perfect work and not ours (which could never be enough). He also came to reveal how God provided a way through his sacrifice so we don't suffer the condemnation we deserve for our sins. Instead Jesus bore all of our shame, guilt, and condemnation on the cross.[6] Mind-boggling.

The Holy Spirit

Earlier in the gospel of John, Nicodemus, a religious leader, visited Jesus under the cover of night, because he saw Jesus as a teacher of God. Jesus shocked him by saying one must be born again to see the Kingdom of God; a person's spirit must be reborn of the Spirit (see John 3:1–21). It wasn't a physical rebirth. Implicit in what Jesus said was: I am the Son of God and the Son of Man, who comes to offer eternal life (defined as relationship with God *now and forever*). No one, not even a respected religious leader like Nicodemus, could bridge the gap created by his sin between himself and God.

When I came to faith as a child after reading a Gospel tract alone, I understood it meant eternity with God. But I didn't know Jesus also gave me his Spirit to live within me and to empower me to live the life he wanted for me. But over the decades, I realized more and more the truth of what the

44

apostle Paul meant in Galatians 2:20; he identified with the crucified Christ so the life he lived was not his own. Instead the resurrected Christ lives in and through him each day. The key is whether we will die to our old way of being and embrace our new identity and life in Christ. Only by grace can we learn to rely on the Spirit and not on our own strength.

The result of identifying with Christ's sacrifice on the cross was that Paul's old inner life (for example, what he once based his identity on apart from God) died. Before identifying with Christ's crucifixion, Paul based his identity and worth on his many accomplishments and heritage. And as Paul also identified with Christ's resurrection, Paul was spiritually reborn with Christ's life within him. Paul no longer lived for himself; Christ changed Paul's desires (see Colossians 3). Christ *restored* Paul's connection with God and gave him God's Spirit (see Ephesians 1:13–14).

Following Christ doesn't mean living a perfect life but our character should be growing more Christ-like. Christ's life within us and His Spirit is — slowly but surely (as we cooperate) — *transforming* us to become more like Christ in our desires, thoughts, and deeds (see Romans 8:28–30 and Philippians

1:6)). It happens in our daily choices—big and small—in our relationships, at work or play.

As you read the gospel of John, I invite you to observe how Jesus interacted with people. He broke cultural and racial taboos by speaking to the Samaritan woman at the well (see John 4:1–45). Jesus said he was the Son of God, which caused the religious leaders of his day to seek to kill him (see John 5:17– 24). Jesus promised to give his followers a Helper, the Holy Spirit of truth, who would be with them and in them after he left (see John 14:15–17 and John 16:13).

Jesus didn't leave us with the option of believing he was only a good moral teacher because a good teacher doesn't claim to be the Son of God if he isn't. As C.S. Lewis once observed, Jesus was either a liar, a lunatic, or he really was the Son of God come in the flesh as he claimed (see John 14:6,9).[7]

Test whether Jesus is the Son of God

One way we can test whether Jesus is the Son of God is if we're willing to do the will of God (or as J.B. Phillips writes in *Your God is Too Small*: "co–operate with the purpose" of God—which is to first love God then others.)[8] Jesus challenges us to know whether his teaching is from God by first practicing the truth of what he teaches (see John 7:16–18). This test applies *before* faith in Christ and it also applies *afterwards*. Often God won't reveal more truth to us until we first do what we already know he has called us to do. For example, God calls me to love him and to love others. Whenever I seek to love God and others (as God leads) by giving my time, attention, and money to another in love, I experience God's Presence anew.

For example, volunteers (from different churches) run a worship service for a sub-acute center's wheelchair-bound patients. The volunteers from my church asked me to teach several times. Once after I taught, I held a white-haired woman's hands while she shared how her husband changed after he fought in World War II. I couldn't take away her pain, but I could listen. God's love (between us) felt as real as her hands in mine.

Whenever I hoard God's gifts to me, I experience less of God's love and peace, although his love for me remains steadfast. God is Spirit and I experience him in my spirit. I turn from unloving behavior because I desire an unhindered connection with God's Spirit.

I change because God already loves me, not to earn his love (see 1 John 4:7-21).

Jesus rules out, as J.B. Phillips writes: "arm–chair critics of Christianity and any dilettante appraisal of its merits."[9] I struggle more often to do what I already know God has called me to do than with a lack of knowledge. When I admit and experience my own brokenness and failure to love well, I see in vivid contrast God's tender love and grace welcoming me back home. He calls me to rest my weary head on his chest. I don't need to live by my own limited strength. Instead, God invites me to be yoked to him and to find rest for my soul (see Matthew 11:28–30). Jesus invites me to abide [or be at home] in him as he abides in me (see John 15:1–5).

To connect with God is to abide in God like we abide at home, or when we visit a friend at his or her home. We sit and talk, or we may also share a meal. *Relationship with God, not productivity, is the goal.* Yes, our actions change because of our relationship with God but that isn't the primary focus. We focus on the root, our relationship with God, then the fruit (our lives) will naturally change.

An essential part of us becoming exceptional— connecting with our extraordinary God to be our best—is to let Jesus transform us through a spiritual rebirth. And once we're "spiritually reborn," we are spiritual babies and need to grow spiritually. We will need spiritual milk, such as reading the Bible and relationships with spiritual mothers and fathers. And God gives us a new family of brothers and sisters. Our unity is based *not* on blood, gender, similar interests, skin color, politics, or socioeconomic status, but on our relationship with God as our Father through his Son Jesus Christ. Our unity is based on our eternal connection with God. If you have been reborn through God's Spirit, then we are siblings in God's eternal family. Welcome sister! Welcome brother!

Journal Questions

"I am the way, and the truth and the
life. No one comes to the Father except
through me."

— Jesus, John 14:6 (ESV)

1.   When you read John 8:1–11 aloud, what strikes you about the woman's situation? What do you observe about Jesus's response? What do you notice about the religious leaders' attitude and response, before and after Jesus asked his question?

2.   If you were in the crowd (see John 8:1–11) witnessing what happened, what would you have thought or done? Who do you relate to most in the story?

3.   Try writing a letter, poem, or song to Jesus about what you think or feel about his interaction

with the woman and the religious leaders. If you're more visually or musically inclined, express yourself in media of your choice. You can dance or create sculpture. Share what you create with another person.

4. When you read the book of John and observe how Jesus treated people and how he lived his life, what stands out for you? What kind of person does Jesus seem like? What makes Jesus smile? Become angry?

Read with an open heart and mind, and try (though it is hard) to leave behind your preconceived notions about God, which may have developed in childhood and taken hold based on input from the media and religious institutions or leaders. *God is infallible, but fallible people often claim to represent God and end up misrepresenting him.* It can be confusing. Savor the stories of Jesus as you read the book of John. Ask the Holy Spirit to enlighten you. Ask for the grace to be and do as your spiritual eyes are opened. It may take a few hours, several days, or weeks to read through and contemplate the gospel of John. (Or you could try reading the gospel of Mark.)

5.   When you read the story of the Samaritan woman by the well in John 4:6–42, what do you notice? How does Jesus embody grace and truth in his conversation with the woman? What truth about himself does Jesus want to reveal to her? What truth about her does Jesus reveal? How does she respond to Jesus at different points during their interaction?

In that culture, men didn't speak to female strangers and discord existed between the Jews and the Samaritans. Jesus broke social and cultural barriers when he spoke to the woman.

6.   What we let in through our eyes, ears, and senses affects how we see Jesus; therefore, it is worth asking ourselves these questions: Are we seeking God in our reading material, music, and relationships? Does what we read online, listen to on iTunes, or watch on Netflix or social media, increase the fruit of the Spirit (such as love, joy, and peace), or does it cause us to be ungrateful, jealous, or resentful and judgmental?

7.   What is one way you can rely on the Spirit instead of on your own strength today? For

example, you could pray about a situation and ask for the Spirit's guidance and help—before charging ahead alone. The Holy Spirit enables us to know Jesus and his ways better (see John 16:13). To walk by the Spirit is *not* about trying harder. It is about admitting we can't do it alone, so we need the Spirit's help. We learn—by trial and error—to abide in God so his Spirit can flow unhindered through us (see John 15:1–5). It means we constantly turn to God and say, "I trust you. I need you. Thanks for being here." It's a *process*.

What kind of reminder can you create to help you to turn to God instead of yourself throughout your day? Something visual? Audio? Tactile? I write Bible verses on index cards. (I know: old school.)

Prayer

"He [Jesus] said to them, 'Come and
you will see.'"

—John 2:39a (ESV)

Dear Jesus,

Thank you for embodying grace and truth. You tell
the truth about me to set me free to live in your
grace and forgiveness.

Please help me to be aware of how past
experiences or others influence how I see you,
others, and myself in false ways. I confess I have
also let my unacknowledged biases and sins cloud
how I see you.

Thank you for the story of the woman caught in
adultery and how you showed her and the religious
leaders both grace and truth.

You cannot restore what is broken if I won't
admit it is broken and needs your healing and grace.
Grant me the grace to be real so you can heal.

Please help me to be open and responsive to

what you show me today. Please give me the grace to trust your unconditional love for me.

Thank you for how your truth sets me free to grow and change.

Please give me the grace to see myself as both broken and beloved in light of who you really are— even when it is hard. Help me to see others and myself with your compassion and truth.

Please give me the grace to desire change where needed. Give me the grace to see that how you made me is a gift. And please grant me the grace to connect with you so I can learn to be exceptional in the ordinary things of life to your glory and our joy.

In your name, amen.

DAY 4

Discern Your Soul's Condition

"We are always being cultivated."

—Susan S. Phillips, *The Cultivated Life*

I stare at the hard brown dirt surrounding a wilted potted plant. Can I make up for my neglect by watering it? I pour some water on it and watch as liquid pools on the dirt like on a glass plate. It doesn't immediately absorb like well-watered soil, accustomed to receiving what it needs. If I keep watering the soil regularly, it will eventually adjust and absorb more easily, and if it isn't dead, the plant will revive.

The soil softens and becomes more receptive to water over time. Like the plant, when our hearts are parched and cracked, we can soften them by watering them with God's Word and presence through prayer. We open ourselves to God's living water. When we're desperate, the best prayer is, "Help." Praying the psalms, like Psalm 23, 34, 37, 42, 63 or 103, has given me words when I had none. Other times I sat quiet before God. And on occasion, a song expressed what I couldn't articulate.

God is endlessly creative in how he speaks to us. But are we listening?

How can I tell if my soul has hardened?

I'm impatient with my family and myself. My mouth utters words that toughen the lines of communication between my spouse or my daughter and me. I focus on what I lack instead of count blessings. I compare and feel jealous. I run from God and toward busyness or food. I ignore God.

We each have different sin struggles, so your hardened soul may look different from mine. Maybe you spend extra time at work (or in ministry) to avoid developing healthy relationships. Or maybe you fixate on improving your appearance or acquiring the latest and greatest technology, in hopes of gaining more of whatever rocks your world. And maybe it does rock your world—temporarily. Maybe you stuff yourself with ice cream and cookies or you reach for your drug of choice to numb your pain. Or maybe you run toward anyone who needs you or will validate you in the moment. You do anything but slow down and speak honestly with God about your life, feelings, and soul ache. You run. You hide.

I have run from God and toward productivity as a way to ease my soul's disquiet. It never quite worked—in the long run. Productivity meant I accomplished my to-do list and more. I wore my busyness like a badge of honor. My worth and identity were based on what I did instead of my relationship with God. Or sometimes, I ran the other way and escaped with TV in the evening to numb my heart's ache.

We can't be exceptional—*connecting with our extraordinary God to be our best*—without discerning the condition of our individual soul. We ask ourselves: is my soul feeling parched or wilted? Many of us don't value or practice listening to our bodies or our souls till something dramatic happens; this was my story. Or maybe we don't know how to value or identify our emotions. God wants our souls (which includes our emotions) to connect with him. Emotional intimacy is part of true connection.

Take one small step

However we've strayed, we can take one small step back toward God. Like the father in the Parable of the Prodigal Son (see Luke 15:11–24), God looks for and responds to even the slightest twitch toward him.[10] When I realize I've wandered, I pray: "Jesus, come for my heart," or "Help me." And God always responds (though not always when or as I expect).

God promises if we seek him with a whole heart, we will find him (see Jeremiah 29:13). We make time for what nurtures our soul; it might be a walk with our phones silenced. We enjoy the sun's warmth, and we observe the birds and the trees around us. We slow and breathe deep. Or maybe we allow ourselves another life-giving activity. What nurtures each of us may differ. And as we water our souls daily with God's Word and his gifts, we begin to sense his light shining on our hearts and lives, showing us the path back to God. Step by step.

My soul has felt broken and unable to hear God's voice in the past for different reasons. Sometimes I didn't know why. In some seasons, unresolved and unacknowledged pain formed a thick, high wall, keeping me from accurately hearing and seeing God. Other times, it was sin. It has also happened when I've overcommitted myself and said, "Yes," to time-consuming activities and obligations at church, work, or school when I should have said, "No, thanks." I didn't know to value myself enough to say, "No." As a recovering people pleaser, I didn't know it was okay to say "no."[11]

Or I said "No," to an opportunity to help at a local event or talk with a loved one about a difficult issue, when courage would have said, "Yes." Part of learning my worth and my calling has been to discover the power and value of saying "no" to what isn't God's best for me. When I say "yes," to what isn't God's best, then by default I say "no" to God's best for me.[12] The more I rest in God's love for me, the more I'm free to say "no," and not worry what others think of me or if I'm missing out. God's love sets me free from the chains of letting fear of others control me.[13]

Before I planted anything in my yard, I removed numerous pebbles and rocks from the soil so my new seedlings could grow unhindered. My head, heart, and soul had stones embedded in them, too, like those lies about my self–worth and fear—they kept me from risk and relationship. In short, those rocks prevented the garden of my life from flourishing.

Possible rocks in our souls

One of the biggest rocks is this lie: We must earn God's love and forgiveness. Unconsciously, many people—even those who believe by faith Jesus paid the price for their sins—believe a lie: God loves us more if we're good and do what pleases God, whether it be service, daily prayer, or living perfectly. (We live differently because Jesus abides in us, but we don't live differently to earn his love and favor.)

We change because God already loves us, not to earn God's love.

For most of my life, I unconsciously believed this lie: God loved me more when I excelled and loved me less when I failed. I missed out on the freedom of resting in God's love when I believed the above lie about God. I treaded water around God when I could have floated on my back and relaxed in his oceanic love.

The Gospel enables us to be exceptional—*connecting with our extraordinary God to be our best*—in the ordinary things of life because our love and acceptance come from God as gift, not because of our performance. We did nothing to earn his love (see Romans 5:8). We can't do anything to lose his love—whatever happens in our marriage, our jobs, or our families. Nor can we do anything to make him love us more than he already does. Although we may experience the consequences of our or another's mistakes, our status as "Beloved" in God doesn't change (see Romans 8:31–39). We can rest in God's unchanging love for us. Astounding.

We can learn to live our lives flourishing more and more in the freedom of his unconditional love.

We seek to be exceptional out of gratitude to God, not to earn his love and favor. God's love is a grace gift (see Ephesians 2:8–9). Let's remove these lies so the soil of our hearts can grow healthy thoughts and fruit. Let's take out the rock of performance–based religion and replace it with the true Gospel of grace.

Lately, I pray: "God, help me to know myself as beloved. Show me how to love others so they also know they're beloved."

God can and often does bless obedience to his ways, but we don't obey God to manipulate him to do our bidding. *God isn't a cosmic vending machine where we get what we want if we put in the right coins.* We can't control God. (If we're honest, we try—to varying degrees—to shrink God to a controllable deity, a false idol.) We obey God because we trust his unconditional love. When we obey God, we acknowledge he is worthy of our trust and gratitude because he first loved us and gave us his best: Jesus, his beloved only Son (see Romans 5:6–8 and 1 John 4:9–10).

The true Gospel of Grace

How can you tell if you believe the Gospel of grace or this lie that we obey God to receive his blessing and love? You'll find clues in your reaction when life doesn't go as you expected or wanted though you've been "good." Do you become angry and bitter? Cut off relationship with God and anyone associated with God? Grow angry because unknowingly you believed God owes you for your service, or you feel entitled instead of grateful? If you react in those ways, or you don't really believe all is grace and a gift from God so you can't earn any good gift from God (see James 1:17), you may believe the lie that obedience to God results in his love and blessing (*as determined by you, not God*). If so, you need to embrace the Gospel of grace.

Another rock (or lie) is: We can sow disobedience to God without reaping what we sowed—that we can sow seeds of hatred and reap love, or we can sow seeds of gossip and lying and reap close friendships. Like a loving parent, God lets us choose to rebel and experience the natural consequences (see Galatians 6:7). But God also forgives and restores when we cry out to him, seeking to change (see 1 John 1:8–9). I've experienced this again and again. Like those who believe God's blessing and love are entitlements, people who believe the lie that they will *not* reap the seeds they sow, can also find freedom in the Gospel of grace.

God honors us with the freedom to choose to follow his way or go our own way.

Removing weeds from my garden

Besides eliminating rocks, I also pulled weeds so my plants and flowers can flourish. Have you ever tried to pull out a large, long weed with your hands? I have tried and failed. The weed's brown roots went so deep, they broke before I could yank them out. If a weed's roots aren't removed, it reappears, spreads, and chokes out the good plants trying to grow. Likewise, for many years, I didn't realize how the *weed of ingratitude* choked out the joy God wanted to grow in me. I gave thanks for some things but failed to give daily thanks for many blessings I took for granted: access to clean water, the Holy Spirit's presence to guide and comfort me, and God's provision of food and shelter.

After I read Ann Voskamp's insightful book *One Thousand Gifts*, I began to record God's gifts to me in a gratitude journal. So far I've counted over 9625 blessings. Each time I thanked God, I planted a seed of joy.[14] My joy grew the more I appreciated God's biggest and best gift to me: Christ (see Romans 8:32) and all my blessings *in* Christ (see Ephesians 1-3). Dietrich Bonhoeffer rightfully observed: "In ordinary life we hardly realize we receive a great deal more than we give, and that it is only with gratitude that life becomes rich."[15]

The *weed of unbelief* also grew long and deep. Now when worry causes me to disbelieve God's promise to care for me, I pray, "I believe. God, help my unbelief," (see Matthew 6:21–34).

Grief and forgiveness

Other big weeds I've had to deal with are unresolved grief and the desire to forgive without fully understanding the process of true forgiveness. I recommend Lewis Smedes' book *The Art of Forgiveness*, a thin paperback thick with wisdom.[16] For decades, I piled false guilt and shame on myself, but his book offered a new perspective. God kept reminding me through different books, wise friends, his Spirit, and the Bible to be compassionate with myself on this journey of forgiveness. And forgiveness involves a process with grief, tears, and acknowledging the hurt (and often fear) under the anger.

One counselor suggested I stop focusing on "forgiving," and instead allow myself to acknowledge and grieve what happened. To forgive, I had to admit what happened, and how it impacted me. She believed as I allowed myself to grieve, true forgiveness would eventually follow. In *Rising Strong*, Brené Brown also linked forgiveness and grief when she said, "We can't forgive if we don't grieve."[17]

Learning to grieve what we lost or suffered is hard and holy work. The grief process is more like a slow cooker than microwave. It requires courage and grace. We can ask God for the grace to grieve.

Our grief recovery begins when we acknowledge our loss and its related secondary losses. For example, the loss of a loved one includes the secondary losses of no longer creating and remembering enjoyable times together. After I resisted grief work for years, I learned grieving releases more joy in my life. Mystery. *Grief is part of the forgiveness process.*

Forgiveness doesn't mean what happened was

right, nor does forgiveness mean an instant removal of pain—though the pain often decreases and may gradually disappear. Forgiveness also doesn't preclude working with authorities to stop abuse.[18]

Forgiveness and reconciliation are different things; the former is unilateral while the latter is bilateral. Forgiveness can include practicing healthy boundaries to prevent further and repeated abuse. It may also mean telling someone else what happened so healing can occur. Finally, forgiveness means we don't seek revenge; we trust God to square accounts and avenge (see Romans 12:19). God tells us to pray for our enemies and to offer water if they're thirsty (see Romans 12:20). *Only by God's grace.*

Whatever the case may be, we need God's wisdom and discernment regarding future interactions, if any, with those who have been abusive. Depending on the situation and the relationship, our forgiveness may encourage the forgiven person to change. Sometimes. In either event, we can give ourselves the gift of forgiveness. By God's grace, we can choose freedom from our past instead of being chained to bitterness and resentment.

Because of God's grace (unmerited gift), God forgives our sins when we receive that gift in faith (see Ephesians 2:8–9). By God's costly grace, we forgive others because God forgave our sins, a debt we could *never* repay (see Matthew 18: 21–35). And when we forgive others and, if needed, ourselves, we also give ourselves a way to experience greater freedom from our past. We open ourselves to a deeper connection with God.

We may have been unable to prevent what happened in the past, but we can prevent bitterness and resentment from stealing our present and future joy. We can choose to be exceptional—connecting with our extraordinary God to be our best—in the ordinary things of our life. We cannot be our best as God created us if bitterness chains us to the past; I know this firsthand. But by God's grace, we can choose to cooperate with God in the hard but worthwhile grief and forgiveness process.

In certified trauma specialist H. Norman Wright's book *Recovering from Losses of Life*, he acknowledges some losses are monumental (such as the death of a loved one, divorce, or the effects of war or a natural disaster); he also recognizes loss is a normal part of life (like aging).[19] Wright says we each have a choice in our recovery though most of us didn't have a choice in our loss.[20] He highlights how parents teach their children to acquire but often fail to teach them how to grieve losses.[21] Research has shown seemingly normal childhood losses such as "growing up with divorced parents, living with a depressed or alcoholic mom or dad, having a parent who belittled or humiliated you" can cause such children to be twice as likely to be diagnosed with cancer and depression as adults."[22] A child suffers a loss of safety, among other losses, when the child is abused. Interventions (for body, soul, and spirit) exist for recovering from trauma; but the loss and the trauma must first be acknowledged.

Each person's recovery process is unique.

Wright's book shaped how we helped our daughter cope with the death of our beloved dog Jubi, and how my husband and I dealt with our grief. Jubi, a mixed–breed hound, was part of our family for almost fourteen years. After he died, we shared funny stories about Jubi, like how he inspired us to compose songs for him. (We never sang in public. *You're welcome*.) We didn't rush to adopt another dog. Our grief's intensity blindsided us. I've also grieved these losses: secondary infertility, our dream of more children and other losses, and certain relationships.

We need to nourish our souls and remove any rocks and weeds if we want to flourish. The Holy

Spirit, given to God's children, reveals the rocks and weeds in our souls if we ask him to reveal them to us (see John 16:13). When we daily ask God to help us remove any rocks or weeds (see Psalm 139:23–24) as they appear, we're free to be exceptional in the ordinary things with our extraordinary God. When we remove rocks and weeds, we create fertile soil in our lives for the fruits of God's presence, such as love, joy, and peace to bloom.

We can be exceptional when we believe God is enough for us in our work and daily interactions. God is enough for us in the midst of our grief and losses. And in the right season, we can believe our souls will overflow with God's good fruit. We regularly drink God's living water, allowing it to satisfy our soul thirst like nothing or nobody can (see John 4:14; Psalm 42).

Journal Questions

"Sadly, the soul enslaved by sinful acts
cannot be healed if we deny that those
acts are really our responsibility."

–John Ortberg, *Soul Keeping*

1.   After reading Psalm 139:23–24 a few times, you can ask God these questions:

Is there any hurtful way in me?

How can you lead me in your ways today?

What attitudes, words, or actions do I need to change?

How can you rely on the power of God's Spirit to enable you to change and become the best you as created by God?

2.   Do you have at least one or two people who love you enough to tell you the truth about yourself? We need them to reveal both the beautiful and the ugly in us—because it's hard to see the

71

complex truth about ourselves. We want to see the good so we can nurture those things. And we must see the hurtful so we can eliminate what hurts others and us. We also may need to seek help for healing from previously unacknowledged wounds or losses. We can't be exceptional (connecting with God to be our best) in our daily lives unless we nurture the good fruit and pull out the weeds and rocks in our lives.

Who can you ask to help you see your strengths and struggles? List names in your journal as they come to mind. When can you set up a time to ask him or her?

3. What thoughts or quotes from today resonated with you?

4. What is one weed or rock in your soul? In Beth Moore's book *Breaking Free*, she said we must work with God to identify the strongholds[23] (what I call the weeds and rocks) in our soul. Do you need God's help to identify a weed or a rock in your soul? What is one step you can take toward removing it by relying on God's Spirit?

Once we identify a weed or rock, it is a continual process of pulling it out and walking in the truth. For example, I identified the rock (or lie): I had to earn God's love and favor. The more I remind myself of God's unconditional love for me, the more I walk in freedom from people–pleasing and perfectionism. Yes, I sometimes struggle, but less over the years.

Do you need to persevere in walking in God's truth? What is one thing you can do today to help you to walk more in the truth? Maybe ask a friend to pray with you and to hold you accountable? Accountability leads to greater success in walking more often in the truth.

5.   In *Breaking Free*, Beth Moore says, "getting to know the Healer is more important than the healing."[24] What do you think Beth means by her statement? What does getting to know the Healer mean to you? For me, getting to know God as my Healer was part of and continues to be part of my healing and restoration.

6.   What are you feeling today? Is your body communicating your feelings through a tightened chest, a headache, a stomachache, or shallow breathing? Or maybe you can't help smiling and

you just want to thank God? Or maybe you don't know what you're feeling, and you need help to identify what you're feeling?

One way to keep rocks and weeds out of your soul is to be ruthlessly honest about what you're feeling and thinking—with yourself and God. We can be honest because God already knows and loves us (see Psalm 139:1–6). Maybe you're learning to value and recognize your emotions (for example, frustration, joy, sadness, excitement) and thoughts as a first step. Or you may be learning to not deny or minimize your emotions and thoughts. Don't say, "I should feel…" or "I shouldn't feel…" What you feel is what you feel.

Be open and curious about your feelings (which will help you learn to be more open and curious about other people's feelings). God already knows your thoughts and feelings so you can process them with him (see Psalm 139:1–6). He won't flare his nostrils at you. Nor will he condemn you.

One of my biggest struggles is to not "should" myself but to simply acknowledge my true feelings and trust God won't condemn me. As I grow in this skill, I also grow in my ability to extend that same compassion to others. Your relationships benefit (in the long term though it may be bumpy in the short term) when you're honest with God and yourself. Where have you been "should-ing" yourself? Write about it and then acknowledge your true feelings before God.

When I'm first honest with God about my true feelings, it makes it easier for me to then share my feelings with another. It also makes it easier for me to allow others their feelings and to not feel like it is my job (*which it isn't despite what some may say*) to try to "fix" them. This is an area of continual growth for me.

7.   What's your response to Tim Keller's statement: "Fear-based repentance makes us hate ourselves. Joy-based repentance makes us hate the sin."[25] What sin or false belief is God calling you to repent of? How can you repent in joy because you don't need to fear losing God's love because you've erred?

8.   What is one step you can take today to walk in greater freedom from a rock (a lie) or weed (for example, unresolved grief, or ingratitude) in your life? Write it down; tell someone else. Remember,

you will progress if you keep walking step by step with God. Don't compare; each person's path is unique.

Prayer

"We tend to use prayer as a last resort,
but God wants it to be our first line of
defense. We pray when there's nothing
else we can do, but God wants us to
pray before we do anything at all."

—Oswald Chambers, *My Utmost for His
Highest*

Father God,

Thank you for empowering me to walk in freedom from any rocks or weeds strangling the good growth in my soul. Help me to see the good seeds and fruit you nurture in my life.

Please show me what rocks or weeds need to be removed from my heart and life. Replace any lies I believe about your character and my worth with the truth. And enable me to believe you want me to flourish and I can flourish.

Thank you for your loving presence as we remove the rocks and weeds hindering my experience of abundant life *in* and *with* you.

Please give me the grace and strength to cooperate with you as we eradicate the rocks and weeds from my heart and life. Help me to remember I must regularly pull weeds and rocks out of my heart and life this side of heaven.

Water the soil of my soul with your unconditional love, grace and truth. Help me to be exceptional in the ordinary things of life as we work together for your glory and our joy.

In the name of Jesus, amen.

DAY 5

What Trials Can Reveal

"If we're to develop a familiar
friendship with God, we cannot
separate ourselves from Him during
pain or temptation."

—Jan Johnson, *Enjoying the Presence of
God*

I couldn't believe she was finally here as I cradled
her tiny body close to me. She felt warm in my arms.
I inhaled her scent and admired her ten little fingers
and tuft of thin black hair. After the heartache of
infertility, she was born. When the epidural wore
off, an acute stabbing pain shot upward from my
sacrum every time I sat and nursed her.

My doctor prescribed a little Vicodin to take the
edge off the pain. But I stopped after two days
because I worried about her receiving it in my milk.

So each time I sat and nursed her, which could be from ten to thirteen times a day, I focused on her latching onto my breast and not on how much it felt like sitting on the tips of sharp spears. Soaring joy mingled with searing pain.

Our Lamaze class never mentioned this type of pain—but then it also never mentioned the legs shaking during delivery. I felt pain each time I sat for a few years though with less intensity.

When our girl was about eight to ten weeks old, she began to sleep a four-hour stretch at night, so my sleep lengthened to allow dreams. I began to awaken at night with my heart galloping like a horse straining toward the finish. I never watched slasher movies where one flees a Freddy Kreuger–like character—and yet in my dreams I ran for my life with the same degree of terror. In all of my nightmares, someone chased me while I raced for my life.

I lay in bed, unable to return to sleep; my husband slept soundly next to me. The streetlight peeked through the shutter's slats, casting shadows on the wall. The house quiet, our baby deep in her own dreams, I couldn't get up and risk waking her, but I dreaded returning to sleep. Besides, soon enough she'd cry and need to be nursed and diapered. In those wee hours I fought those nightmares and during the day I battled anxiety, which always bobbed above the surface like a beach ball I kept pushing below water.

Seeking help

For over a year, I suffered in stoic silence, *unaware* of my patterned response. Finally, after three older women I respected and trusted encouraged me to seek help, I phoned a counselor. I wanted to sleep without night terrors again. I wanted to move through my days without adrenaline surges and my chest tightening.

My time in therapy revealed several lies I believed about God. One key lie: if God loved me, then my life would be easier. I also unconsciously believed this lie: God would punish me if I felt or expressed anger, even if hurt and fear were underneath the anger. My felt belief didn't include God being open to all of my feelings (such as, anger, hurt, and frustration). I didn't uncover the lie's *decades-long root* until a counselor helped me uncover what caused my sudden recurring nightmares, depression, and intermittent panic, and anxiety attacks.

To my disappointment, I learned a decades-long

root couldn't be removed in a few months, nor would it be fully eliminated in a few years. (But its hold could be weakened). I clung to God and his promises like seeds of new life and hope. I fought to believe in the promise of spring (see Psalm 126:4).

As part of my healing journey, I met with a Christian counselor and for a short while, I also met with a doctor. Their diagnosis: depression and PTSD. The finding of depression didn't surprise me, but the PTSD diagnosis did; I thought only veterans suffered from it. While veterans often have a more severe type of PTSD, anyone who survives trauma can exhibit similar symptoms. The doctor recommended I read Dr. Robert Karen's book *Becoming Attached* to gain new understanding.

This trial didn't resolve quickly, although the nightmares did lessen and disappear after several months. My underlying depression and anxiety took much longer to diminish, because it was like an old shoe, easy to slip into unaware.

Excavating toxic beliefs about God and myself took years. If you've ever tried to untangle a ball of yarn, you know how it can get worse before it gets better. At times, I despaired of ever improving. Throughout, God allowed me to see new vistas and beauty as I trudged uphill toward recovery. Step by step; or, more accurately, three steps forward, two steps back. Slowly and painfully, I shaved off decades-thick layers of lies and hurt—sometimes balking and resisting, but making progress—only by God's grace.

I feared if I began the journey, my long-buried emotions (and implicit memories) would tsunami over me and I'd drown. But God assured me of his promise to never abandon me (see Hebrews 13:5). I also had to fight this lie: it was selfish to address the pain. The counselor kept reminding me if I denied or ignored my pain, it didn't reduce another person's pain. Plus, pain kept me from being fully available to my loved ones. She also invited me (again and again) to examine my memories and feelings *without* condemnation or shame. I had to learn to identify some of my feelings. We met regularly at first then sporadically as I stabilized. God graciously provided funds and babysitters.

We didn't meet for a few years. Then my anxiety resurfaced during the day and sometimes at night. I awoke with my mind racing, lost in a labyrinth of fear. God kept nudging me to uncover more layers for deeper healing. I resisted. But God kept prodding me toward greater flourishing. I found a new Christian counselor (as my first one retired) to unearth why anxiety and fear kept cropping up like weeds. We met periodically. She helped me to better understand what caused my anxiety. She often reminded me to be compassionate toward myself. She reiterated: I was doing all I could; I couldn't make my healing happen faster. *Sigh.* She suggested I keep inviting God to be *with* me in the midst of my anxiety and pain. I also prayed more (alone and with friends) because of the spiritual dimension to my battle.

Whenever I surrendered to God's timing and ways, I would gradually feel more at peace and less anxious. Sometimes it happened without my awareness until I realized I wasn't holding my breath. It was like a slow sunrise pushing back the dark cover of night.

Our extraordinary God wanted me to be exceptional in the ordinary things of my life, which included parenting, writing, teaching, and marriage. I define "exceptional" as "connecting with God to be my best," and by "best," I mean "more fully myself as God created." I couldn't be my best if I didn't address hidden pools of hurt and fear, bubbling up in unexpected anger or anxiety when triggered by criticism (real or perceived), or disappointment. God wanted greater wholeness for my soul. *Each of us has our own unique best as God created us with different gifts.* For example, what is exceptional in a writer is usually not what is exceptional in a software developer although they may overlap.

I couldn't be fully the person God created while unresolved grief occupied space in my soul. Once more, God called me to more grief work. Again I balked, until by God's grace, my desire for wholeness overcame my resistance.

Redemption

Almost thirteen years after my first appointment with a counselor, I see more of God's redemptive goodness toward me as he drew me closer to his heart. He showed his tender, compassionate heart toward me in different ways. God also gave me new compassion for certain individuals' brokenness. He *transformed* the primarily intellectual truth of his unconditional love for me as revealed through Christ's sacrifice so it became more of a heartfelt truth — *theology incarnated in experience and not only as creed.* The Bible became more real. God's love also became more like loving arms around me than a painting I admired from a distance. As I emptied myself of more lies about God and myself, God filled me with an increasing sense of his deep indescribable love for me (see Ephesians 3:14–21).

Imagine a bottle full of gunk with a foul smell and appearance. You empty the bottle first if you want to replace its contents with something fragrant and lovely. If you don't, the gunk will always contaminate whatever is added to the bottle. And so it was with my soul. I needed to remove the lies and the pain so I could experience more fully God's *nonperformance-based love* for me. God restored my ability to connect with him on a more intimate level.

God didn't want me to know him the way a child learned the alphabet by rote. He desired me to learn his love language until it went beyond my head and was absorbed into every nook and cranny of my soul like my mother tongue. God desired me to create poetry with him. It's a *lifelong* process.

I am prone to picking up lies like my dog's fur picks up burrs. As I must regularly brush my dog, I need to daily ask God to reveal what's in my heart. Every day, I require his help to see him, others, and myself through his lens of love. And daily I must brush away the lies and replace it with truth.

How our brain processes pain

If our daughter's birth hadn't triggered painful emotions and memories, I wouldn't have known or believed how buried pain can grip and shape a person. In retrospect, God's severe mercy allowed me to break so he could restore me.

Since the brain takes the pattern of a previously painful experience (trauma has an even stronger hold) and overlays it onto a current event, the past affects how you perceive today's stress or pain. *Today's pain can trigger yesterday's unresolved pain.* Your brain does this without your conscious awareness. The brain is wired to seek patterns. Even if a patterned belief may not be correct—especially if the pattern formed during early childhood when the brain can't fully reason yet—your brain won't be able to tell what is true and what isn't. You correct a false patterned belief by consciously examining the belief later, often as an adult, if you couldn't earlier.[26]

Comfort received then given

This trial also taught me the truth of God's promise to comfort me so I could then have the privilege of comforting others with the comfort he'd given me (see 2 Corinthians 1:3–4). I've seen this circle of redemption surround others and me during struggles. Because God comforted my inner child, I comforted a friend's inner child with the truth of

God's love. I told her it wasn't her fault when she was bullied at home and at school; she was *only* a child and couldn't control her circumstances— although as children, we try. The adults in her life failed to protect her even when they knew of her suffering. And she and I unconsciously carried that childhood pattern into adulthood until God revealed the destructive pattern to us. And when we broke, God healed and reformed us to greater emotional and spiritual health.

We revisit those old patterns—not to wallow in the past or to cast blame—but so we can recognize and reject those patterns, and replace them with healthier ways of living and loving. Remember my first empty the bottle of gunk analogy? We discard the lies we believed and replace it with God's love and truth about us. We partner with God in our restoration process. We create new healthy beliefs then practice living them.

When we experience greater emotional and spiritual health, then we can be exceptional in the ordinary things of our life as we connect with our extraordinary God. We also seek to help others live in greater freedom.

Jesus suffers with us

No one escapes suffering in our broken world. Sadly, some suffer inordinately when others use God's gift of free choice to inflict harm. And no one has suffered more injustice and physical, spiritual, emotional, and psychological suffering than Jesus (see Hebrews 4:15–16 and John 19). Jesus suffers with us and he knows like no one else what we feel. When he most needed his friends, they abandoned him. Only a few women, including his mother, and the apostle John stayed with him while he died naked and shamefully like a criminal on the cross — though he committed no crime. Because Jesus rose from the dead, we never ever suffer alone. Jesus never abandons us (see John 20; Hebrews 13:5). *We're always held in love.*

Sometimes God's comfort is palpable and feels as close as a loved one's arms wrapped around you. Other times, God feels strangely distant and you feel like a ship lost in the fog, unable to see the beacon from a lighthouse. God, like the lighthouse, continues to beckon us to safety nonetheless. Even when we feel adrift in a sea of hardship, God, like the lighthouse, has not moved. If you're feeling lost and forgotten, do not give up. Cling to God and his promises. *Remember the cross and not your circumstances are the measure of God's great love for you (see Romans 5:8).*

The more I contemplate Christ's crucifixion and resurrection, the less my circumstances sway me toward unbelief of God's love for me. It's okay to wrestle with God; remember Job. Depending on my response, trials can either draw me closer to God or further (see James 1:2–4). It's a *lifelong process* of learning to trust God.

If you call God your heavenly Father, he is with you as his Spirit is within you. You are never alone. You can call to him for help.

Daily I call to God for help (see Psalm 121). I have sensed God's presence closer than my breath and other times, I only recognized his presence in the rear view mirror.

In a life of faith, we will experience *both* his presence and his apparent absence. If by God's grace we persevere, our faith, trust, and intimacy with God deepens despite our suffering. And as our connection with God strengthens, we can be exceptional in the ordinary things of our lives with our extraordinary God.

Journal Questions

"The root choice is to trust at all times
that God is with you and will give you
what you need."

—Henri Nouwen, *The Inner Voice of
Love*

1.   When you read 2 Corinthians 1:3–4 aloud several times, what words or phrases resonated with you? What is one way you can take a word or phrase to meditate on throughout your day whenever you have a free moment? For example, could you type it into a note on your phone to review as you wait in line or before your next meeting, or write it longhand?

2.   Can you recall a time when God or someone else comforted you? What did you feel and think? How have you been able to come alongside someone else because of a similar trial you experienced?

3.   What makes it hard for you to believe and receive God's comfort?

Ask God to remove any obstacles or lies about him and yourself so you can experience his comfort and love for you. (If you didn't receive comfort for emotional distress when you were growing up, then you may not know what it feels like to have someone accept, love, and hold you in your distress without judgment or shame. I highly recommend Milan and Kay Yerkovich's web site, www.howwelove.com and their free resources, such as a list of Soul Words/feelings and journaling prompts to become more self-aware at https://www.howwelove.com/resources/.)

4.   How has God's comfort not looked like what you expected?

In the book of Ruth, when Naomi lost her husband and two sons, God provided Ruth to help and comfort her. But Naomi couldn't see Ruth's true value as God's gift until later. Can you relate to Naomi? I can. Keeping a gratitude journal helped me grow in seeing God's gifts as I regularly record God's blessings (such as his promises in the Bible). When you look back, can you see how God provided a "Ruth" or somehow helped you during a crisis? If not, can you ask God to help you see how he did provide? Sometimes it takes years to see and sometimes we won't know till heaven.

5.   Can you relate to what I shared earlier of how I suffered in stoic silence for over a year (unaware of my patterned response) before seeking help for my clinical depression, nightmares, and anxiety attacks? Do you need to reach out to friends and helping professionals for support? Please don't suffer alone because of feeling shame over needing help. There is no shame in getting professional counsel and treatment. We can't be our best when we're wounded and need help.

6.   If you're not in the midst of a trial and you know someone who is, how can you encourage and comfort that person today? Send a note? Text? Call? Visit? Bring a meal? Offer to listen without giving advice?

7. How can we worship God in lament as modeled by many of the psalms (for example, Psalm

22, 42, 69, and 73? If you wrote a psalm to God, what would you write?

In many of the psalms, David honestly cried out to God with his anguish, pain, and questions but then he reaffirmed his trust in God and his goodness. But the Bible also includes Psalm 88, which ends in darkness to acknowledge how we may feel at times. Worship doesn't mean we wear a fake smile before God. Worship helps direct our eyes back onto God instead of our problems. And when we can't worship, God still holds us close.

Sometimes trust is turning our gaze and our broken hearts toward God without words.

Sometimes I pray a prayer written by Ruth Myers in her book *31 Days of Praise*. Ruth lived her prayers when she became a young widow with children after her first husband died of cancer. In *31 Days of Praise*, Ruth reminds me true worship surrenders all to God in trust. What helps you worship God? What helps you trust God? What is one way you can worship God today?

Learning to worship God aright is a lifelong process.

Prayer

"So let us come boldly to the throne of
our gracious God. There we will
receive his mercy, and we will find
grace to help us when we need it
most."

—Hebrews 4:16 (NLT)

Our Loving God,

We praise you for how Jesus understands all of our weaknesses and he faced all the temptations we have (in kind) yet he didn't sin. We praise you because we can boldly come before you for the grace and mercy we need *without fear or condemnation*.

We praise you for being a God of all comfort and for your Holy Spirit's constant presence within us. Please give us the grace to believe and receive the comfort you long to give us.

We surrender our tears and fears into your compassionate and tender hands.

Thank you for not wasting our tears or fears. As Christ rose from the dead, you can bring new life out of what feels like death to us.

You are a God of hope (see Romans 15:13). Enable us to abound in hope.

We thank you for your comfort and for how you redeem our pain by allowing us to be part of your healing presence to another.

We ask for the grace to trust you enough to cling to you when we or our loved ones suffer. Thank you for how you hold onto us and never let go. Thank you for how you give us grace for the moment when we ask for it. Please give us the grace to seek your face instead of straining in self-effort. May we rely on your grace to be exceptional in the ordinary things of our lives as we live, work, and love.

In the name of Jesus, amen.

DAY 6

Take Steps Toward God

"Grace, we must learn, is opposed to
earning, not to effort."

—Dallas Willard

I used to think The Parable of the Prodigal Son was only about the younger son, the so-called prodigal who squandered his inheritance, then when he was at his lowest feeding pigs, came to his senses (see Luke 15:11–32). Now I know the dutiful son, who stayed at home, was also a prodigal.[27] When the story began, the younger son couldn't wait to leave home and his father. But when he was starving, dirty, without friends, and hungry for greasy pig slop, he recalled his father's servants ate enough. Far from being exceptional, he decided to return home and ask to be a servant to earn his keep.

The father saw his son first, picked up his robes, exposed his legs, and ran toward the prodigal. By doing so, he bore his son's shame and protected him from the villagers' wrath.[28] According to their first century culture, an older man didn't bare his legs, but the father's actions prevented the villagers from stoning the prodigal. The father embraced and kissed his son, ignoring the swirling stench of pig, sweat, and dirt. The father showered him with extraordinary grace, mercy, and love.

The father owed his son nothing; his son owed him everything. But in his great love, grace and mercy, he gave his son a fine robe to replace his filthy rags, a ring for his dirt–encrusted finger, and shoes for his blistered, bleeding feet. The rich robe, ring, and shoes signified he was the father's son and not a servant. No need for his son to eat with the servants—the father restored him to his position as son. What an extraordinary father!

The father threw a big party to celebrate his son's return. The prodigal didn't reject his father's undeserved generosity out of pride. When the prodigal's older brother returned and discovered the reason for the party, he refused to join. The oldest felt he had served the father and deserved a party more than the prodigal. He felt embittered against his brother and father. Again the father humbled himself by going outside to entreat his oldest son to join the celebration. The father assured his oldest everything he owned also belonged to the oldest son. The story ends without telling us whether the oldest son came in, but it's clear though he stayed at home, the oldest son was a prideful prodigal at heart. Neither son appreciated their extraordinary father and the depth of his love for them. Neither son chose connection first with the father.

Where do you find yourself in the story?

When Jesus told this story, his audience included two groups: the tax collectors and sinners; and the Pharisees and scribes. The religious leaders were upset at Jesus for eating and spending time with tax collectors and sinners. The prodigal represented the tax collectors and sinners. The older brother represented the Pharisees and scribes, the religious elite. The loving father represented God, who wanted both groups to receive his joy and be in relationship with him and each other.

Whether we identify more with the dutiful, resentful older brother or the wild- living prodigal, God invites us to receive relationship with him. But we each must accept his invitation to join the party. When I was a young child, I thought choosing the invitation only meant asking Jesus into my heart and receiving his gift of forgiveness for my sins. I thought leaving the Father would be wild and sensational.

Now I realize it's possible to leave our Father God in daily choices. When I choose resentment over forgiveness, or condemnation over community, I leave my Father's loving presence. I easily forget my heavenly Father's heart toward me is one of unconditional love. I forget God gives me all my heart truly needs. Leaving God isn't always about dramatic sins.

God lets me choose: I can run away and reject relationship with him by busying myself with duties or immersing myself in pleasures. Either way, I live far from him; either way, my heart leaves its true home in God.

Whenever I fail to appreciate God's holiness, love, and extraordinary grace toward me, I can easily become like the older son and feel entitled to more than God has given me. I can forget God has given me *all* in Jesus (see Ephesians 1). When I am ungrateful, I become alienated like the oldest son. I compare and get jealous. The older son based his identity on his "good works," and *not* on his relationship with his father.

Or I can be like the prodigal and seek affirmation and life apart from God, even in something good like service to court the approval of others. Whenever I realize I am trying to earn God's love and acceptance, when it is already mine, I go to a "far country," like the prodigal. Far from home, I forget God's love isn't based on my performance, my worthiness, or another person's approval. I forget only God's love meets my heart's deepest longings. I forget my heart's true home is with God.

I travel away from God whenever I forget I have all I need in him and instead seek my soul's fulfillment elsewhere.

Far from my heavenly Father's heart, I cannot cleanse the evil thoughts and desires fighting within me. Like both sons, I forget my greatest treasure isn't external and won't be found apart from my Father. When I recall my greatest gift is my Father's love, grace, and presence within me, I come home. God promises to provide all my needs through his riches in Christ (see Philippians 4:19). God gives me his Spirit to empower me to live the life God calls me to live. My weakness can be a portal to strength when it is surrendered to God (see 2 Corinthians

12:9–10). When I remember God's promises and true character, I begin the journey home.

When I, like the prodigal, admit I can't change myself or my situation, I open myself to receive God's grace. When I confess my need, I begin to walk home. As I bask in Father God's loving presence, he changes me, bit by bit, from the inside–out (see 2 Corinthians 3:18).

I return home to God's presence when I cry to God for help to forgive and love certain people instead of attempting to pull myself up by my emotional bootstraps. I return home when I profess my deep spiritual poverty apart from God. When I cast off the dirty rags of pride and embrace humility, I return home to God's loving welcome.

Some of our earthly fathers (in their humanity) loved us conditionally while others failed to love us at all. Still some had fathers who loved them in a healthy way. Regardless of our experience, all of us have God as a heavenly Father who delights in us, welcomes us, and longs to hear from us.[29] Before we turn to him, his loving eyes search for us. God responds to our cry for help (see Psalm 107). He forgives us and celebrates our return as sons and daughters. God removes our filthy rags and clothes us with Jesus Christ's wholeness and right standing before him (see Romans 8:1–17). He calls us his sons and daughters.

We find what our heart most longs for at home with God. Recall I defined "exceptional" as connecting with our extraordinary God to be our best. When we return home to God's heart of love and connect with him, we can be exceptional in the ordinary things of our lives.

Journal Questions

"For thus said the Lord God, the Holy
One of Israel, 'In returning and rest
you shall be saved; in quietness and in
trust shall be your strength.' But you
were unwilling."

—Isaiah 30:15 (ESV)

1.   What touches you about the Parable of the Prodigal Son when you read Luke 15:11–32? The prodigal ran from his father and wasted his inheritance. The older brother remained out of duty but not love for his father. Which brother do you identify with more and why?

2.   Do you envision God looking for you every day, waiting for your slightest move toward him? The father looked daily, scanning the horizon for the prodigal's return. Can you let your need draw you home to God's heart of love?

In faith, you can choose to believe that God will

not condemn you. God seeks to embrace you in welcome and forgiveness (see 1 John 1:7–9). What is one way you can return to God by opening yourself to God's grace? Will you ask God for the grace to behold his gaze of love seeking you?

3. Where have you seen God's grace in your life? If you're having trouble seeing God's grace in your life, ask God for the grace to see and believe in his grace. Be willing to risk being open to his grace, knowing he is not like those who may have abandoned or wounded you.

4. What does it mean for you to believe God sees you dressed in Christ's goodness instead of stained by sin (though you're imperfect)?

Just as the father took away his prodigal son's filthy clothes and gave him new ones, God takes away the filth of our sins and clothes us with Christ's righteousness (see Romans 4:5–8; 5:17), if we believe and receive Christ's death and resurrection on our behalf.

105

5.   What is one thing you can do today to claim and live the truth of 2 Corinthian 5:17 (in Christ, you're made a new creation)?

Your past is not your identity. *Shame or fame is not your true name in Christ.* God gives you in Christ a new identity—as his beloved daughter or son. It takes a lifetime to fully implement and live into *all* the implications of your new identity but your new identity is yours the moment you believe in Christ's work on the cross for you. Ask God for the grace to believe and receive more fully your new identity in Christ.

6.   What is one way you can make reading the Bible a regular part of your day? Reading the Bible is one key to knowing God better. Think of it as God's love letter to you so you can know your new family better. Maybe you can download a Bible reading app like Bible Gateway or Blue Letter Bible? I highly recommend subscribing to Timothy Keller's Gospel in Life podcast. Join a small group Bible study?

I often learn more when I study God's Word with others (after first studying alone), because I benefit from their insights. None of us can experience the richness of our Trinitarian God's character apart from community. We need each other's unique perspective.

7. How do you view God as Father? Do you need to ask God to reclaim and restore the word father in your life? Vine's Expository Dictionary of New Testament Words says the word "Father," (Greek: pater) comes "from a root signifying 'a nourisher, protector, upholder."[30] For some of us, the word "father" triggers painful memories and we need to ask God to reclaim and restore our image of father in light of our relationship with him. We must not let the darkness we've experienced overcome the light of God's love. God's light through Christ has overcome the darkness (see John 1:4–5). God is the Father who delights in us, always welcomes us, and longs to hear from us. Nothing is too trivial, too big, or too shameful to share with him. Ask God to give you the grace to see and experience him as the good and loving Father he is.

8. How does experiencing a famine (or any desperate need)—like the prodigal did when far

from home—then remembering God's welcoming love motivate us to return to God? God's gracious love is bigger than any of our failures. What would change if we really believed God celebrates when we return home to him? How would we live if we believed God always looks and longs for us to return to him?

9.   If you left God for the far country, what is one step you can take to return home? If you're not sure what step to take, ask God to show you. Then when he does, take that step. (God won't ask you to do something contrary to what is revealed in the Bible, which is why it is important to know what the Bible says.) Share your step with at least one supportive and safe person today.

10.   If you haven't left home for the far country, what is one step you can take to stay close to God's heart? If you're not sure, ask God to show you then be prepared to act.

11.   If you're close with God, at home with him,

what is one thing you can do to help another return home? Ask God to bring someone to mind or help you show kindness to someone today.

Prayer

"God's love in the face of our
wickedness is what awakens us to
humility and contrition."

—David Roper, *Psalm 23*

Our Father God,

I praise you for your tender heart for me. I thank you for how you long for me to be near you, and you grieve when I wander. Please give me the grace, hope, and courage to walk back to you when I travel to the far country.

Thank you for how you celebrate my homecoming no matter how far I've run. Thank you for how Jesus bore my shame, guilt, and sin on the cross. Thank you for the new life I can have because of Christ's resurrection and ascension.

Please forgive me when I don't turn to you for the rest and love I desperately need.

Forgive me when I turn instead to food,

entertainment, or any other form of numbing (work, drugs, illicit relationships, etc.) as a way to avoid vulnerability with you. Please forgive me when I seek fulfillment away from you. Thank you for how you don't give up on me but wait for me with love in your heart and eyes.

Please give me the grace to stop striving for my worth apart from relationship with you. Give me the grace to rest in my identity as your beloved child. Help me to rest, knowing you want to give me good gifts in your time.

Thank you for giving me the *immeasurable* grace gift of relationship with you, now and forever.

Please give me the grace and strength to entrust myself to you and receive your loving wisdom and care.

Thank you for seeing me clothed in Christ's righteousness no matter how I fail because of Christ's work on the cross for me. Thank you for restoring me so I can be exceptional in the ordinary things of life for your glory and our joy.

In the name of Jesus, amen.

DAY 7

Rest and Play

"Our bodies and souls are unified. If
our bodies suffer, so do our souls. We
cannot neglect the body in pursuit of
spiritual growth."

—James B. Smith, *The Good and
Beautiful God*

Many years ago, when I worked as a lawyer at a
large law firm, my forearms began to ache when I
performed daily actions such as shifting gears on a
manual car or brushing my teeth. It suddenly hurt
to cut food and use chopsticks; my forearms
throbbed with pain at night and disrupted my sleep.

I ignored the pain for about a month before I saw
a doctor. It wasn't until about a year-and-a-half later
that I saw the right type of physical therapist—one
with expertise in treating chronic repetitive strain

injuries in the hands and forearms. What you don't know can hurt you. She told me my pain was now chronic, but she would try to ease it. From then on, whenever people I knew had a similar injury, I urged them to seek the right medical help immediately and to take their injury seriously.

Fast forward to 2016. I don't have constant pain, but I have experienced painful flare–ups when I pushed past my body's warning signs. (Or when I ignored the pain because life required me to, such as when I cared for our girl as a newborn and toddler.) In retrospect, my body told me what my mind didn't want to accept: my job at the law firm was a bad fit for my soul and body.

Many of us ignore or deny our need for sleep and rest. I've been guilty of this, and I'm working on sleeping more. A sobering thought: "According to a study by the AAA Foundation for Traffic Safety, people who sleep six to seven hours a night are twice as likely to be involved in such a crash as those sleeping 8 hours or more, while people sleeping less than 5 hours increased their risk four to five times (italics added)."[31] Wow. People who sleep less than 5 hours increased their risk of a car crash four to five times *because of sleep deprivation induced inattentiveness.* Lack of sleep not only hurts us but it also increases our potential to harm others.

Sometimes we can't sleep because we're caring for a newborn or a sick family member, or we stay up late to meet a deadline for work or school. Once the emergency or deadline is over, we allow ourselves to rest. Or if circumstances don't allow for regular rest, we may need to get creative—for example, we could form a babysitting co–op—to get the rest we need. But we must respect, whenever we can, how God made our bodies to need sleep. In general, around eight hours is optimal. For most of us, the process of sufficient rest ebbs and flows.

Research shows inadequate sleep causes weight gain more easily and increases our odds of developing obesity, diabetes, and cardiovascular disease.[32] In short, lack of sleep also causes our emotional and physical health and well–being to suffer. In contrast, sufficient sleep enables us to work, love, and create art at our best. We need adequate sleep to be exceptional in the ordinary things of life.

We can trust our extraordinary God to hold our lives together as we sleep.

What we need beyond sleep

Beyond sleep, we also need time for recreation—or,

shall we say, rest by playing. Remember how play came naturally as a child? How productivity was the last thing on our minds? This is another soul–care practice that has taken me many years to more fully embrace. When my patience and resilience disappear faster than watermelon on a hot summer day, I can often attribute it to lack of sleep or a need for restful recreation.

I try to exercise at least three to four times a week, even if it is only a short walk and a few quick stretches. I allow myself to read a book for pleasure and not merely for growth. I make time for silence because I must be still to know God (see Psalm 46:10). Without solitude and silence, the loudest voices (external or internal) can easily drown out the Spirit's whisper to me. In midlife, I recognize it is not selfish but wise to practice self–care so I can be exceptional—connecting with our extraordinary God to be my best in my relationships and work.

Mother Teresa advises: "We all must take time to be silent and contemplate, especially those who live in big cities...I always begin my prayer in silence, for it is in the silence of the heart that God speaks. God is the friend of silence—we need to listen to God because it's not what we say but what He says to us and through us that matters."[33]

Many of us live electronically connected almost 24/7. The idea of five minutes of silence may seem impossible. For others who have practiced and experienced the gift of silence, five minutes may seem too short. In his book *5 Pounds*, Harley Pasternak tells his clients to unplug from all electronics (for example, tablet, phone, laptop, and video games) at least one hour each day.[34] Inspired in part by Pasternak's recommendation, I take a break from social media one day a week and limit my time on social media daily. Currently, I don't have alerts set for any social media apps on my phone, but I admit this may change.

Start where you are and begin with one step. At first, you may find yourself grabbing for some gadget to fill the silence—in that moment, stop, take a deep breath, and ask God for the grace to be still and silent. To aid as a focus in your silence, you may pick a short prayer, such as "Grace to trust," or "Thy will be done." Exhale. Look for openings in your day. Maybe you'll find five minutes during your morning shower or commute. Or maybe you'll go to bed earlier so you can wake up earlier. Ask God to show you how you can creatively arrange your day so you can experience time in his presence. God answers when our heart cries out for more of him.

Don't give up if you fail. Expect to be challenged—again and again. Get back up and try anew with God's help. Enlist a friend or group of friends to be your accountability partner(s). Share with one supportive person or, better yet, invite them to join you on your quest to practice silence and solitude with God.[35] When I embarked on a forty-day social media, TV, and movie fast, I invited my blog readers to join me. [36] Thankfully, a few did.

In her article "How Solitude Can Change Your Brain in Profound Ways," Jane Porter "urges people to create sacred spaces where solitude can be embraced, and where you don't allow yourself to check your phone or reach for distraction—an hour every morning, or a lunch outside the office."[37]

Whenever I ask God for the grace to spend more time with him, he always answers. Often he surprises me. It makes life an adventure. I never know what divine appointments God may have for me. Sometimes I miss these divine gifts because I'm not looking, or because I look for an open door when God has instead opened a window.

God longs for us to trust him enough to rest. We don't need to carry the weight of the world—or our lives, or the lives of loved ones—on our shoulders. *God's shoulders can carry the burdens we were never meant to shoulder.* Our inner selves need rest as much as, if not more than, our bodies. And our bodies can't fully rest if our souls keep straining for worth.

Now that I've experienced the benefits of silence and solitude with God, if I go for more than a day without some silence, the world screeches like fingernails on a chalkboard, and my ability to love well suffers. My friends who exercise daily tell me if they skip a day, they can sense it—in a bad way. Likewise, I've experienced the benefits of a regular time of silence and prayer, so my soul craves that time when it gets crowded out. My soul thirsts and needs the living water only God can provide (see Psalm 42:1–2). After fighting my need for quiet and rest for years, I've learned it is okay to respect and honor how God designed me. And even with that newly formed craving for time alone with God, I appreciate reminders of how good and wise it is to make time for silence and solitude.

If we aren't already doing so, we may also need to create space to be with friends and loved ones. Research shows healthy social connections also contribute to our health and longevity; so when we connect with others, it isn't a luxury. Rather, we live in community as part of a well–lived life.[38] God as Trinity exists in community (Father, Son and Spirit), and since God created us in his image, we also need community to thrive.

It isn't selfish to make time to care for our minds, souls, and bodies. We can't love others well when we're constantly tired. When Jesus lived on earth, he modeled time with friends, service to others, and also time alone with God in prayer. If Jesus in his humanity practiced care for himself, how much more do you and I need to practice self–care!

If we want to be exceptional, defined as connecting with our extraordinary God to be our best, we must each care for our respective body. And remember "best" is *not* about comparison but about being most fully ourselves with our unique strengths. We need sufficient rest to be our best.

Our bodies, souls, and minds are how we show up for work, play, and relationships. Whether we're aware or not, our bodies affect our ability to love and live well. So we need to nurture our minds, souls, and bodies through rest, solitude, and community to be exceptional in the ordinary things of life. And as Oswald Chambers reminds us, it won't be learned in five minutes. In midlife, I'm still learning to make room for these healthy practices in my daily life.

Journal Questions

Now may the God of peace himself
sanctify you completely, and may your
whole spirit and soul and body be kept
blameless at the coming of our Lord
Jesus Christ. He who calls you is
faithful; he will surely do it.

–1 Thessalonians 5:23–24 (ESV)

1.   What is one lie you believe about sleep and rest? (For example, I don't need adequate rest to be my best, or it's not important.) What truth can you replace the lie with today? And how can you put that truth into practice today?

2.   What is one truth you can focus on today as incentive to change your lifestyle so you can experience more rest? For example, God determines your worth, not your work or achievements, so you can rest from excessive work as a way to prove your worthiness.

3.   What is one step you can take to ensure you get adequate rest? For example, be in bed by 10 p.m.—a goal I aspire to reach more often. Write it down. Share it with another person, like I did. Easy, right?

4.   What is one way you can play this week as part of God's gift of rest to you? Go for a hike? Read a book for pleasure? Garden? Play basketball or a board game? Paint? Bake? Whatever it is, it needs to be enjoyable—and productivity can't be a goal.

5.   What is one thing you can do to practice internal rest from striving for worth today? I highly recommend Timothy Keller's sermon/podcast, "Work and Rest." In one of the best—if not the best—teachings I've heard on work and rest, Keller shows how we need inner attitudes toward rest before we can fully rest on the outside.[39] What do you think of the idea of resting internally from striving for worth as a prerequisite to allowing oneself to rest externally? Can you relate? How so? If this is hard for you, you can ask God for the grace to learn to rest.

Prayer

"We imitate God by stopping our work
and resting."

—Peter Scazzero, *Emotionally Healthy
Spirituality*

Our Father God,

I praise you for how you modeled rest after the work of creation. I praise you for how fruit trees have seasons of rest between times of fruitfulness.

Thank you for the gift of rest from striving to earn your love and acceptance because of Christ's life, sacrifice, resurrection, and ascension. I thank you for giving me intrinsic worth so I don't have to prove my worth.

Thank you for how you created me with a body, soul, and spirit made to rest—thank you for wanting me to rest. Forgive me for not taking seriously your invitation and gift of Sabbath rest.

Empower me to entrust my body, soul, and spirit to your care.

Help me to learn to trust you enough to rest, cease working, and engage in what I enjoy as a gift from you, without guilt or shame. Give me the grace to believe you are enough and who I am is enough.

Forgive me when I believe the lie that you are not enough, and therefore the person you created me to be is not enough.

Show me how to find and create moments of rest in your presence daily and each week. Show me how I can celebrate in community as part of the regular rhythm of my life.

In your Son's name, amen.

CLOSING THOUGHTS

"It is ingrained in us that we have to do exceptional things for God—we do not. We have to be exceptional in the ordinary things of life, and holy on the ordinary streets, among ordinary people—and this is not learned in five minutes."

—Oswald Chambers, *My Utmost for His Highest*

Dear Reader,

Congratulations, you made it! Thank you for joining me for seven days of knowing God and his love more deeply so he can do the extraordinary with your ordinary. You can be exceptional—defined as connecting with God to be your best—in the ordinary things of life. *Your best is being who God created you to be; it isn't about comparison and competition.* Your best is unique to you. Every act you do with our extraordinary God isn't ordinary — it's exceptional because it is infused with his holy presence. Christ lives in you (see Colossians 1:27).

Don't listen to the lies whispered by the enemy of your soul about your worth. You fight an ongoing battle, but God gives you the armor you need to stand firm. You only need to put on the armor — *daily,* through prayer (see Ephesians 6:10–18). You can call on God's Spirit to enable you to stand in God's love, truth, and grace. I do. Every day.

Please don't follow Christ alone. God designed us to live our fullest and best life with him and in community. We flourish together but we will flail and fail alone.

The apostle Paul reminds us, "To set the mind on the flesh [old nature apart from God] is death, but to set the mind on the Spirit is life and peace" (Romans 8:6 NRSV). The battle begins with our thoughts, so we must intentionally curate what we look at online and in print, what music we listen to, and what we think about, because it all starts in the mind. Our thoughts are seeds bearing fruit in our words and actions. ("For as he thinks in his heart, so is he [in behavior]" Proverbs 23:7a (AMP)).

Speak God's promises to your soul (like David in

Psalm 103). Refuse to listen to the father of lies about your worth and hope for the future.

Remember: God helps us when we ask. God designed us to be our best as we rely on his Spirit, grace, and love. *We can be exceptional as we connect with our extraordinary God throughout our day, whether our task is mundane or marvelous.*

God's faithful love and mercies are new every morning, so today is a blank canvas to paint on with God (see Lamentations 3:22–25). Put your hope in God and begin anew. Don't let yesterday's failure or success keep you from continually seeking God. He always desires to connect—his Spirit with your spirit.

God created you in his image so you have intrinsic worth. Don't let your worth depend on what other people think of you, or the lies you may unconsciously believe. Your worth is not based on your possessions, power, or performance (good, bad or middling).

You can use your gifts to bless others. God gives you all you need to "be exceptional in the ordinary things of life" as you connect with his Spirit and love (see John 15:5).

Holley Gerth encourages us:

"You are not who you were yesterday,

You are not who you will be tomorrow.

You're in the middle of the beautiful process of becoming."[40]

I pray this little guide serves as a portal to increasing intimacy with God, our greatest present and eternal treasure.

Join me as we keep taking one step at a time with our extraordinary God. What an honor to write our story within God's greater story. Don't give up. To help you continue in your journey, I include a list of recommended resources at the end of this book. See if one of these resources might serve as a companion in the weeks ahead. Invite a friend to join you.

Once again, thank you for joining me as we learn to be exceptional—*connecting with our extraordinary God to be our best*—in the ordinary things of life. What an exciting lifelong journey!

Keep painting on your life's canvas to create a masterpiece with the Master Artist.

Please keep in touch via SoulStops.com (my blog) or on Instagram @DollyMLee or #7DaysofSoulCare .

RECOMMENDED RESOURCES

On soul care/deeper intimacy with God

- The Holy Bible
- A.W. Tozer, *The Pursuit of God*
- Brother Lawrence, *The Practice of the Presence of God*
- Peter Scazzero, *Emotionally Healthy Spirituality*
- James B. Smith, *The Good and Beautiful God*
- Ruth Haley Barton, *Invitation to Solitude and Silence*
- Susan Phillips, *The Cultivated Life*
- Jan Johnson, *Enjoying the Presence of God*
- John Ortberg, *Soul Keeping*
- Ann Kroeker, *The Contemplative Mom*
- Laura Boggess, *Playdates with God*
- David Roper, *Psalm 23: Hope and Rest from the Shepherd*
- Emily Freeman, *Simply Tuesday*

Daily devotionals

- Timothy & Kathy Keller, *The Songs of Jesus*
- Peter Scazzero, *Daily Office: Remembering God's Presence Throughout The Day*
- Sarah Young, *Jesus Calling*
- Mark Batterson, *Draw the Circle: The 40 Day Prayer Challenge*
- Ruth Myers, *31 Days of Praise*
- Oswald Chambers, *My Utmost for His Highest*

Online resources

- http://www.gospelinlife.com
- https://www.blueletterbible.org/
- https://www.biblegateway.com/
- http://howwelove.com (Learn your love style and how to improve your relationships)
- https://renovare.org/articles
- https://renovare.org/podcast
- http://www.thetransformingcenter.org/
- http://www.timothykeller.com/blog/2008/8/1/the-importance-of-hell

Other recommended resources

- Beth Moore, *Breaking Free*

- Timothy Keller, *The Reason for God: Belief in an Age of Skepticism*
- Mark Labberton, *Called*
- Brennan Manning, *Ruthless Trust*
- Milan & Kay Yerkovich, *How We Love*
- Holley Gerth, *You're Already Amazing*
- Milan & Kay Yerkovich, *How We Love Our Kids*

ACKNOWLEDGEMENTS

With my heartfelt gratitude to all who have enabled me to practice soul care:

I thank God for rescuing me from the pit of despair many times and giving me a new song to sing. *I owe everything to you.* Thank you for loving me with your steadfast unconditional love and grace. All praise, honor, and glory to you.

Brian, thank you for twenty-five years of friendship, laughter, and marriage. Thank you for persevering through the valleys with me. This book exists because you kept encouraging me to write. Thank you for the *countless* ways you help me.

Our dearest daughter, you are God's precious gift to us. I always thank God for who you are and who you are becoming.

Karen and Kirby, thank you for over twenty-two years of friendship, faithful prayers for our family, and being our daughter's godparents.

Debbie, thank you for twenty years of friendship, and serving as midwife to the birth of this book with your words and prayers.

Ann Kroeker, thanks for believing in this book's message and for your expert edits during its development.

Judy, Kim, and Mary, three wise women in ministry, thank you: this book and my healing wouldn't have happened without your love, wisdom, and friendship during a critical juncture.

Thank you to the community at Peninsula Bible Church for being part of our faith journey for over twenty-two years.

Thanks to the healing prayer ministry of the Silicon Valley Healing Rooms of Prayer, Sunnyvale, and the House of Hope, and their prayer warriors.

Thank you to each friend who prayed for me as I wrote. *You are my partners.* Thank you to each generous friend who read draft versions and gave me invaluable feedback.

Thank you to each friend who helped launch this book. You are a grace gift.

And a special thank you to the readers at Soul Stops for being a kind community and for engaging with me on issues related to our relationship with God. Your prayers, emails, and blog comments have brightened my soul many a day.

NOTES

¹ "Vincent van Gogh on achievement," Quotations Book, accessed July 11, 2016, http://quotationsbook.com/quote/201/.

² Emily Freeman highlighted this Oswald Chambers quote in her encouraging book *Simply Tuesday* (Grand Rapids, MI: Revell, Baker Pub. Group, 2015), 39.

³ Will Haskell, "People are searching for a woman who donated a rare Apple computer worth $200,000 to a recycling center." *Business Insider*, June 1, 2015, accessed July 1, 2015, http://www.businessinsider.com/recycled-apple-i-computer-2015-6.

⁴ James Bryan Smith, *The Good and Beautiful God* (Downers Grove, IL: Intervarsity Press, 2009), 38.

⁵ I exercised creative license with some of the details but not with Jesus's words (see John 8:1–11 ESV).

⁶ The apostle Paul wrote about God's grace in Ephesians, and Romans, among other books of the

New Testament. He wrote from personal experience. Paul (formerly Saul) once based his worth and identity on his accomplishments, heritage, and religious credentials (see Philippians 3:4–9). Before his conversion, Paul watched with approval as men stoned Stephen, a leader in the early church, till he died a bloody death (see Acts 7:54–8:3). He eagerly sought to persecute Christians as he entered "house after house" dragging men and women and putting them in prison (Acts 8:3). Can you imagine what these men and women experienced as they were dragged from their meals or their beds? After Paul met Christ on the road to Damascus, he met with Ananias, who helped in his conversion. From then on, Paul's view of himself, Christ, and other Christians changed forever as his zeal was now to proclaim Christ and the Gospel (see Acts 9:1–22).

7 "I am trying here to prevent anyone saying the really foolish thing that people often say about Him: I'm ready to accept Jesus as a great moral teacher, but I don't accept his claim to be God. That is the one thing we must not say. A man who was merely

a man and said the sort of things Jesus said would not be a great moral teacher. He would either be a lunatic — on the level with the man who says he is a poached egg — or else he would be the Devil of Hell. You must make your choice. Either this man was, and is, the Son of God, or else a madman or something worse. You can shut him up for a fool, you can spit at him and kill him as a demon or you can fall at his feet and call him Lord and God, but let us not come with any patronizing nonsense about his being a great human teacher. He has not left that open to us. He did not intend to." C.S. Lewis, *Mere Christianity*, "C.S. Lewis Quotable Quote," *Goodreads*, accessed September 21, 2016, https://www.goodreads.com/quotes/6979-i-am-trying-here-to-prevent-anyone-saying-the-really.

[8] J.B. Phillips, *Your God is Too Small: A Guide for Believers and Skeptics Alike* (New York, NY: Touchstone, an imprint of Simon & Schuster, 1952), 84.

[9] Id.

[10] Timothy Keller shared how a woman in his congregation, complained she had prayed over and

over, "God, help me find you," and nothing happened. Finally, a "Christian friend suggested to her that she might change her prayer to, 'God, come and find me. After all, you are the Good Shepherd who goes looking for the lost sheep.'" She said God answered and found her. Timothy Keller, *The Reason For God: Belief in an Age of Skepticism* (New York: Penguin, 2008), 251.

[11] If you want to learn what your love style is, you can take Milan and Kay Yerkovich's free Love Style Quiz at their website Howwelove.com, accessed July 14, 2016, https://www.howwelove.com/love-style-quiz/.

[12] During editing, I was reminded of Lysa Terkheurst's book *The Best Yes*, which I didn't read but heard about a few years ago. It sounds like a wonderful book.

[13] And I need God's grace to not pick up those chains again. But when I do, I can always ask God for forgiveness, repent, and begin anew.

[14] When it is hard to give thanks, I can thank God for his presence and how he will redeem this trial because he has promised to do so in Romans 8:28-

30. I recommend Timothy Keller's podcast, "A Christian's Happiness," where he does an excellent job teaching on Romans 8:28-30, dispelling some common misperceptions about what those verses promise, available at http://www.gospelinlife.com/a-christian-s-happiness-6506.

[15] "Quotes by Dietrich Bonhoeffer," accessed July 15, 2016, http://www.quoteland.com/author/Dietrich-Bonhoeffer-Quotes/1640/.

[16] Do *not* get Lewis Smedes's first book on forgiveness. His second book reflects his changed perspective.

[17] Brené Brown, *Rising Strong*, (Penguin Random House Audio, 2015) Audible version, Chap. 47.

[18] One brave friend testified against the man who molested her when she was twelve. Her testimony also exposed the man's sexual abuse of his daughter.

[19] H. Norman Wright, *Recovering from Losses in Life* (Grand Rapids, MI: Revell, 2006), 21–39.

[20] Wright, *Recovering from Losses in Life*, 118.

[21] "Unfortunately, most adults are unable to help their children grieve because they have never

learned to properly grieve themselves. When a child doesn't grieve over a loss, a similar loss in adult life can reactivate the feelings associated with the childhood experience. Thus a childhood loss can predispose us to oversensitivity and depression." — H. Norman Wright, *Recovering From Losses in Life*, 11.

[22] Donna Jackson Nakazawa, "Childhood Trauma Leads to Chronic Illness—so why isn't the medical community helping patients?" *ACES Too High News*, August 10, 2016, accessed September 7, 2016, https://acestoohigh.com/2016/08/10/childhood-trauma-leads-to-lifelong-chronic-illness-so-why-isnt-the-medical-community-helping-patients/.

[23] Beth Moore, *Breaking Free: Discover the Victory of Total Surrender* (Nashville, TN: B&H Publishing Group, 2000), Kindle edition.

[24] Moore, *Breaking Free*, Kindle ed.

[25] Timothy Keller, *Counterfeit Gods: The Empty Promises of Money, Sex, and Power, and the Only Hope that Matters*, "Timothy Keller Quotes," Goodreads, accessed July 18, 2016, http://www.goodreads.com/author/quotes847789.Timothy_Keller.

[26] See generally Daniel J. Siegel, M.D., and Mary

Hartzell, M.Ed., *Parenting from the Inside Out: How a Deeper Self-Understanding Can Help You Raise Children Who Thrive* (New York: Penguin Group, 2003).

[27] I read Henri Nouwen's book *The Return of the Prodigal* many years ago. He introduced the idea of the older brother as also being a prodigal to me. However, I did *not* rely on or peruse his book for my examples of when I act like a prodigal with God. I studied the Parable of the Prodigal with the Spirit's help.

[28] See section titled, "Middle Eastern Village Context" of Joan Huyser–Honig's, "Kenneth Bailey on Jesus through Middle Eastern Eyes," accessed January 9, 2016, http://worship.calvin.edu/resources/resource–library/kenneth–e–bailey–on–jesus–through–middle–eastern–eyes/.

[29] You can watch, see, or listen to a dramatization based on Scripture of the "Father's Love Letter to You", *Father's Love Letter*, accessed August 2, 2016, at http://www.fathersloveletter.com/.

[30] Vine's Expository Dictionary of New Testament Words, Dictionary Aid section, *Blue Letter*

Bible, accessed July 12, 2016, https://www.blueletterbible.org/lang/Lexicon/Lexicon.cfm?strongs=G3962&t=NASB.

[31] National Sleep Foundation, "Facts and Stats" *Drowsydriving.org,* accessed July 12, 2016, http://drowsydriving.org/about/facts-and-stats/.

[32] Dr. Anne E. Rogers, "Sleep and Health," Division of Sleep Medicine, *Harvard Medical School,* January 16, 2008, accessed July 12, 2016, http://healthysleep.med.harvard.edu/need-sleep/whats-in-it-for-you/health.

[33] Mother Teresa, *A Simple Path* (New York: Ballantine Books, 1995), 7-8, quoted by Peter Scazzero, *Daily Office: Remembering God's Presence Throughout The Day* (Illinois: Willow Creek Association, 2008), 4.

[34] Gabrielle Olya, "Celebrity Trainer Harley Pasternak Shares Five Things You Should Do Every Day to Lose Weight." *People.com,* June 28, 2015, accessed July 12, 2016, http://www.people.com/article/harley-pasternak-five-daily-habits-weight-loss-health?.

[35] For ways to practice solitude and silence, I